THE
Salmon
PEOPLE

*This book is part of a series
republished from the original list of Gray's Publishing
in Sidney, British Columbia. We carry the logo from
Gray's on all such books to acknowledge the
contribution made by Gray Campbell, an individual
who began publishing Canadian books in the early
1960s. In the process, he produced a list of
distinguished titles of lasting value to today's reader.*

Gray's Publishing Ltd.

THE Salmon PEOPLE

**25th Anniversary
Special Edition**

Hugh W. McKervill

[signature: Hugh W. McKervill]

Whitecap Books

Vancouver / Toronto

FIRST PUBLISHED BY
Gray's Publishing, 1967

First Canadian Edition 1967
Whitecap Edition 1992

Published by
Whitecap Books Ltd.
1086 W. 3rd St.
North Vancouver, B.C.
V7P 3J6

Cover illustration by Doug Smith
Cover design by Carolyn Deby

CANADIAN CATALOGUING IN PUBLICATION DATA

McKervill, Hugh W.
The salmon people

ISBN 1-55110-017-7

1. Pacific salmon fisheries — British Columbia
—Pacific Coast—History.   2. Salmon canning industry—
British Columbia—Pacific Coast—History.   3. Salmon
industry—British Columbia—Pacific Coast—History.   I. Title.
SH349.M35 1992   639.2'755   C92-091009-2

Printed and bound by
D. W. Friesen & Sons Ltd.
Altona, Manitoba

Printed in Canada

TO KATHLEEN AND MARY

Who were born among
The Salmon People

Contents

INTRODUCTION

The Salmon People was first published in 1967. It was my personal
contribution to the marking of Canada's centennial year. John Fisher,
widely known as "Mister Canada" for his tireless promotion of the national weal, was Chief of the Canadian Centennial Commission for a
time and as such he presided over the approval of a small grant which
enabled me to do some of the research. Later, upon reading the completed work, he expressed the opinion that it was the sort of book that illu-
minated the country's "real history," whereupon he launched into one
of his ebullient discourses on the heroism of the ordinary men and wom-
en who had built the nation. Given such noteworthy endorsement, I suppose one may safely say the book is eminently Canadian.

Actually, the impetus for writing it had little to do with patriotic
fervour. *The Salmon People* is the product of exhilarating personal experience, stimulating research, and lucky timing.

On a brisk August afternoon in 1959, Northland Navigation's flag
ship, the SS *Canadian Prince*. reversed its engines and shuddered into
a slow drift off the village of Bella Bella, three hundred miles north of
Vancouver on Canada's Pacific coast. Weighted down with a couple of
fresh academic degrees, I stepped out of the belly of the steamer onto a
converted gillnetter which had nuzzled alongside and was taken ashore
while the old ship grumbled into motion again, resuming its journey
north to Prince Rupert.

Bella Bella village, at that time, was a smattering of weather-beaten
houses set on cedar stilts driven into the muskeg. The spire of the United
Church rose above the general plane of the mossy roofs, and the white
shingled hospital, owned and operated by the Church, stood out conspicuously, overlooking the channel. A boardwalk running parallel to the

shore laced the whole assemblage together against the backdrop of stunted spruce that clad the hill behind. It was a long way from the ivy-clad granite and the marble arches of academia.

I was there to take up my duties as United Church minister to the one thousand Kwakiutl Indians for whom Bella Bella was home; a role for which six years of university had provided little relevant preparation. I soon discovered that during the summer months most of the men were off fishing and the women were working in the cannery at Namu, three hours away by boat. Only the elderly and the very young remained in the village. So, in order to identify with the people I had come to help, and with a wonderfully ill-informed lust for adventure, I bought a dilapidated old gillnetter and for four summers I went commercial salmon fishing in Rivers Inlet and along the central coast.

On my first night of fishing I managed to wrap the net into the boat's propeller and as darkness receded before a cold misty dawn, there I was, helplessly drifting towards a range of ominous rocks. No aid was in sight. Of course not! Nobody fished in that area, I found out later. There was nothing for it but to strip off my clothes and slide into the paralysing water with a gutting knife to hack the tangle of web and line free from the propeller. That was the first of innumerable misadventures, some of which were uncomfortably close to disaster.

Over time my skills improved and I even managed to catch fish; sometimes a lot of fish. I became smitten with the fever of hope for the "big catch" that is in the veins of all commercial fishermen. I exulted in the magnificence of the ocean and respected its inexorable power. I experienced overwhelming physical fatigue and the luxurious respite of a "mug up" with a fellow fisherman who would bring his boat alongside to sagaciously lament the lack of fish or to wisely wonder at their abundance. In the northern night I stood on my deck and looked into the curtain of blackness, perforated with pin pricks from the mast lights of the fleet. I fished all week and caught barely enough to pay for my fuel and I fished one night and almost sank with the load of thrashing sockeye. I had swollen hands and stinging eyes from the splash of jellyfish slopping over the rollers. I sensed fear being alone in a tiny craft on the swells of Millbank Sound in the all-encompassing night with rain lashing and waves slapping at the planks. And even now, I can smell again the mingled odours of sizzling steak, coffee, fish scales, fuel, and bilge water that hung in the air around the floats where the boats tied up for the weekend and where groups of weather-worn men gathered in wheel-houses to swap yarns and sip from cracked mugs. It was a unique way of life set in an astounding environment and I was living a story that I knew had to be told.

The initial intention was to tell an autobiographical tale of my own adventures. However, as the search to authenticate some allusions to history expanded into months of absorbing research, and as I listened to and recorded the recollections of men and women, many of whom had spent their whole lives up-coast, the project took a different shape. Personal experience is not explicitly part of the content. It undergirds the telling of the much larger story.

The first edition of *The Salmon People* enjoyed success. Reviews across the country ranged from complimentary to paeans of lavish praise. There was one notable exception, however, which resulted in full-blown controversy.

A regionally-noted editorial reviewer for the *Vancouver Sun* took exception to three of the book's conclusions: namely, that the salmon was a fragile resource under stress from overfishing, pollution, competing interests, and human folly; that the relocation of Japanese Canadians from the West Coast during the Second World War had more to do with deep-rooted racial bigotry than with any genuine threat to security; and that the right of Indian people to catch food and to earn a living from a resource with which their life and culture had been inextricably inter-twined from time immemorial was threatened and ought to be protected.

The reviewer's scathing condemnation of these themes drew fire from Farley Mowat, never one to miss an opportunity to speak out on behalf of the underdog and the environment. The ensuing word-battle attained carnival proportions and raged in headlines on page six of the *Sun* for several issues.

The *Sun's* reviewer argued that the Japanese Canadian community was a menace. He wrote, "there may have been graft and injustice in the sale of their boats and land; if so it was regrettable, but a minor feature of the whole operation." Most Canadians are pleased that this line of thinking no longer finds wide support. On September 22, 1988, the

Prime Minister of Canada, in announcing a program of redress, acknowledged on behalf of the nation that the treatment of Japanese Canadians during and after the war was unjust and that government policies of the day were influenced by discriminatory attitudes. It is a matter of considerable personal pride to me that *The Salmon People* said this over two decades earlier.

When it became known that a new edition of *The Salmon People* was to be published I received a phone call from a gentleman attached to the Japanese Canadian Redress Secretariat of the Department of the Secretary of State in Ottawa. He expressed pleasure, as do I daily, that I was still alive and told me enthusiastically that he carried a copy of *The Salmon People* with him in his briefcase and had used it for years as a resource for giving speeches and lectures. He also politely pointed out that the confiscation of property and the relocation had been carried out under the War Measures Act, not the Emergency Powers Act, which came later; that the 189 Japanese Canadian veterans of World War I did not actually get the right to vote until 1935 and that Morikawa was Japanese consul during the race riots in Vancouver in 1907.

The issue of the Indian fishery remains contentious. In a Supreme Court of Canada decision rendered in 1990, the highest court in the land has indicated that the aboriginal right to fish for food is constitutional in nature and that while recognizing the justification of conservation laws, ". . .whatever salmon are to be caught, then priority ought to be given to the Indian fishermen. . ." (R.v Sparrow, No:20311). The matter is far from settled for it remains to determine what constitutes justifiable conservation regulations and what is an appropriate allocation for the aboriginal food fishery, a controversy which in the spring of 1991 brought about nasty demonstrations by non-Indian fishermen. Salmon was traditionally used for barter and formed an integral part of Indian cultural life so the broader question of aboriginal claims to fishing rights for commercial purposes remains a contemporary issue.

The problems affecting the salmon as a resource today are not fundamentally different from twenty-five years ago. Over-capacity of the fleet and environmental pressures remain the main threats to the beleaguered runs of fish.

In an effort to alleviate the pressure of overfishing, restrictive licencing was introduced in 1969. The number of vessels has been reduced from over six thousand when the measures were introduced, to forty-five hundred in 1991. However, the "rule of capture" prevails. No one owns any part of the common property resource until it is caught. This arrangement, besides ensuring a medium for the culturing of conflict between various competing factions, creates pressure to invest in ever more sophisticated gear, and more expensive vessels. No longer can a young fellow venture out with an old boat and a rag of a net hoping to earn a living. A reasonably well-equipped gillnetter and licence today will cost the fisherman a quarter of a million dollars. This is what is euphemistically called a "capital intensive" occupation.

One of the results is that even though there has been a reduction in the number of licensed fishermen the capacity of the fleet has increased substantially. A fraction of the fleet could easily catch all the available fish. Fishing is often restricted to one day per week. For seiners in a given area it might be one twenty-minute opener per week. Were it not for this strict regulation by the Department of Fisheries and Oceans the pressure on the salmon would be intolerable.

The Department's programs of regulation and resource management and the 1985 International Salmon Treaty with United States (up for renegotiation in 1992) must be credited with contributing to some encouraging returns of sockeye and pink salmon in recent years. There are those in the industry who even speak hopefully of a return to historic levels of fish. Maybe! But a few peaks do not make a trend. The Pearse Commission Report of 1982 showed that levels of abundance at that time were just over half of the 1894 to 1913 period. Ten additional years is too short a time upon which to make conclusive predictions. Continuing urbanization and industrialization with their attendant environmental contamination (particularly around the lower Fraser), the exploitation of timber and mining resources, agriculture, hydro power development, and global climatic changes are still persistent threats to the well-being of the salmon stocks.

The industry itself is prone to an extraordinary array of pressures and problems. The growth of a politically persuasive commercial sports industry, fish farming, litigious aboriginal rights issues, free trade, a 1990 GATT ruling permitting U.S. buyers unlimited access to supplies of raw fish provided it is landed at B.C. locations, capricious world prices over which the B.C. industry (producing only about 10-15 percent of the world wild salmon supply) has little control, and the complexities of global economics and world markets, are a few of the more obvious factors which make life ever more complicated and ever more serious for those who count themselves among "The Salmon People" of British Columbia.

If this book provides a historical framework for better comprehension of a fascinating industry built around a mysterious, living resource, I am pleased. In so far as it has managed to put a finger on some social issues which help us understand ourselves better as Canadians, I am gratified. If the reader is able to catch glimpses of the lives of ordinary people, sometimes doing extraordinary things, as they earned a living and made their way through life, then, I am satisfied.

CHAPTER 1

The First Salmon

There was little activity about the camp to reveal the growing tension and excitement, but it was there nevertheless. Even the dogs, mangy, ill-kept critters that lay lethargically on patches of mud outside the shacks, seemed to have one eye partially open in anticipation of the announcement that would start the festivities. Occasionally one would raise its head, sniff the air, jerk into a series of motions designed to get its frame off the ground, then give up as though exhausted and flop its head back onto outstretched paws.

The children would be dismissed once the ritual started, for the Tsimshian people believed their young were ceremonially unclean and never permitted them to attend a "First Salmon Ceremony". Yet, like children of any race, they showed the greatest amount of excitement, running back and forth between the weir and the racks, and from the racks back to the shelters, or out to the high bluff from where the salmon usually could be seen darting in the greenish water below. But the salmon were not running. Not yet.

It was raining. Not very heavily. Just the usual incessant drizzle that saturated the forests, filled the lakes and kept the streams alive with gurgling, grumbling water. In a land where gigantic clouds clambered in from the Pacific to be gouged open on the ragged peaks of the Coastal Range, no one noticed the rain. No one measured it. Rain was as much a part of reality as the mountains that leaped from the water's edge and soared off through heavy timber to thrust their barren heads into those grey clouds. Rain was as sure as the salmon.

But were the salmon sure to come? There were stories of days gone by when the fish had failed to appear on the great rivers, stories borne on the taut lips of hungry people from far up the river of mist, horrible stories of starvation, of mothers with dry breasts, children dying and old men weeping. But in this little clan of Tsimshians, gathered by its ancestral fishing place on the north-west coast of what was to become Canada, waiting for the first salmon of the season, there was no memory of hunger.

Theirs was not a large river, merely a stream that would almost stop running during one of the infrequent dry spells. When that happened the sockeye would mill about in the salt-chuck waiting for the return of the water before they could continue their relentless journey to the spawning beds in the streams that ran into the lake behind the hills.

The salmon of this stream were not as large as those of the great rivers. But they were sockeye — the richest in oil content and the reddest in flesh, and year after year they were there, some seasons more numerous than others, but always providing enough to dry on the racks for winter use and enough to smoke over the smouldering hickory of the smokehouses. Once every four years they came in great abundance. Of course, the shamans of the clan were swift to point out that the salmon's return was due to the success of their prayers, incantations and rituals, for this honoured guest from the sea must be treated with respect or his spirit would be offended and the sockeye would not return to that stream.

Practically everything was ready now. Some of the men were at the weir, carrying large, slimy stones and dropping them into place in the semicircular wall that ran out from the beach. They were making last minute repairs. When the tide flooded the wall would be covered with water. Then as the ebb set in and the water receded through the cracks between the rocks and below the level of the dyke, the fish, if there were any, would be trapped behind the weir in shallow water where they could be speared. On a big-tide the area behind the stone wall would be dry and all the men had to do was to walk out amongst the flopping fish and pitch them with sharp sticks onto the bank where the women went to work, cleaning and slicing them for drying and smoking.

The racks were ready. Some of them had been knocked over by bears last fall or earlier in the spring before the people moved from the winter village. Others had been old and unsafe for the heavy load they had to bear. But they were all repaired now and they stood like some gigantic skeleton along the grassy edge of the beach. Soon these racks would be festooned with thousands of thin fillets of salmon flesh. Behind the racks were the smokehouses and further along the beach towards the bluff were the temporary houses or shelters, a cluster of drab, weather-worn shacks that served their purpose in the summer and were abandoned all winter.

Outside one of these cedar-slab huts sat an old man, with a face like crumpled leather. His gnarled fingers struggled to fix the detachable bone point onto the foreshaft of his harpoon. He did not need to use his harpoon now for there would be enough fish, all being well, from the stone weir, and everyone knew that his fishing days were over. He would be well provided with food. But the old man wanted the feel of the harpoon in his hand — just once more. If he could only spear the first salmon this season he could go to his ancestors in peace. He fought back the frantic feeling of hopelessness as his stiff joints failed to perform. On his weathered face no trace of emotion showed. He was just an old man working with a harpoon point and the envy he felt for the young men as they leaped across the rocks was buried deep beneath ten thousand years of silent stoicism.

The tide rose. Silently it inched its way up the beach covering the debris and refuse left on the stones. It climbed up the face of the stone weir and slid through the cracks. It lapped at the edge of the tule grass and choked the mouth of the stream so

3

that its babbling ceased. The swarthy people on the beach waited and watched. Then it happened!

Splash! There was no mistaking it. Ripples on the placid water showed the spot. Splash! again, and a silver arc cut through the surface, flopped sideways and disappeared.

"Suck-kai! Suck-kai!" The excited yell went up from the boys on the bluff. They were dancing up and down with glee. The men picked up their harpoons. Some went to the stream to stand on rocks, poised and ready to plunge the deadly weapon into the first salmon to show itself for the split second necessary to get in a shot. Others waited till the tide turned and the water receded far enough to enable them to walk out on top of the weir.

"Old man" rose slowly from his position by the opening of the shelter, grasped his faithful harpoon and hobbled toward the weir.

"If only I could spear the first one," he thought over and over to himself.

He took up a position on a flat rock at the edge of the weir where he knew the sockeye would swim past. He was counting on experience to defeat the skill of youth. The icy water made his ankles numb and his robe of goat wool was sodden and heavy with the rain. But he stood motionless, harpoon balanced delicately, as he had done so many seasons before. Only now there was little joy in it, little joy for an old man with pain racing along the chords of his limbs and stiffness sitting in his bones. But maybe he would be lucky. Had he not been a good fisherman these many years? Had he not provided well for his people when his arm was strong and his eye swift to see? Surely nature would be kind to him now and close his years with honour. He would catch the first salmon of the season. He felt sure he would, and the more he thought about it the surer he became, till no longer did he feel the icy coldness about his feet and ankles, and the coarse, wet robe was no more a burden on his back. His eyes narrowed as he peered into the water, looking, waiting for the blue-black shadow of the fish.

4

Stretched out along the little dyke of stones, and stationed at various points by the river were the other men, each one intently watching the water, each armed with his harpoon. A man's harpoon was his pride. It had to be well balanced for accurate thrusting. It had to be strong, yet not heavy. The head must be detachable with a thong leading back to the shaft, for the mighty salmon would soon wiggle free from an ordinary spear. With his harpoon a man might be required to provide the major portion of the winter's food for his family.

"Old man" saw the shadow of the salmon, the flash of the shaft, the explosion of water as the frantically fighting body of silver broke surface and went hurtling through the air onto the bank. But it was not his shaft that had made the thrust. His body was too old, his eye too slow. The young man beside him had caught the first salmon. Now the ceremony would begin.

From the main shelter four shamans trudged towards the spot where the fish had been landed and where it now lay gulping sporadically on the blood-stained grass. It was a handsome creature, bright silver for the most part, blue-green on the back, with touches of olive about the head. The sockeye was admired and treated with great respect by all the Tsimshian people for its beauty and for its generosity in returning year after year to feed them.

Now one of the shamans donned the clothing of the fisherman who had landed the fish. In his right hand he held a carved cedar rattle and in his left an eagle's tail. With these he would keep away all evil spirits. Solemnly the fish was laid on the new cedar-bark mat brought specially for the occasion. Some red ochre and bird's down were spread around the body, then slowly the procession made its way towards the hut of the chief. The shaman wearing the fisherman's clothes led the way shaking the rattle and wiping the air with the eagle tail. "Old man" followed behind the precious cargo. His age was a burden to him at the stream with harpoon in hand, but back at the house he would have a privileged position at the ceremony about to take place.

"Every age has its advantage," he thought, as he passed

5

through the opening into the dim interior of the flimsy summer house.

Some of the women did not come into the house, and none of the young people. Two young mothers with children still nursing stood watching from a distance. They too were ceremonially unclean.

Slowly and solemnly the others filed into the chief's house. It was a plain building of split cedar, nothing like the fine longhouse at the winter village, but adequate for the few weeks spent at the fishing place while the winter's food was caught, dried and smoked.

At last everyone was inside and seated on benches around the smoke-stained interior. In the centre the fish was laid out upon a clean, cedar board with its head pointed in an upstream direction. One by one all the shamans of the village entered wearing their ceremonial regalia, which consisted of bizarre collections of ornaments and charms upon their robes of goat hair and fur. An air of expectancy gripped the people as slowly they proceeded to walk around the revered guest. Twice, three times, four times, they circled the bright fish, sometimes throwing little puffs of bird down in the air or dashing pinches of red ochre about the body, while those watching sang the praises of the honoured one who voluntarily gave itself up to death that they might live, but whose being lived immortally — the supernatural salmon.

The shaman wearing the fisherman's clothing suddenly held up his hand. Immediately there was silence. Two old women approached the salmon brandishing shell knives — for everyone knew that if stone or metal knives were used there would be thunderstorms and disaster.

A deft glance of the shell and the head was lopped off. Thick dark blood smeared the cedar board. The head lay separated from the body, its eyes fixed, its mouth open. Now the other old woman severed the tail. A cut was made along the ventral side and the stomach was removed — and all the time the women mumbled honorary names to the carcase they were dissecting: "Quartznose", "Lightning of the River", "Great Jumper", they addressed it, as piece by piece the fish was cut and prepared for the ceremonial meal to follow.

"Old man" watched with satisfaction. All was right and proper. His disappointment at failing to spear the first salmon had left him now and the tinge of rancour he had felt was cleansed from his mind by what had taken place, even as the tide cleans the beach. He had witnessed and participated in the "First Salmon Ceremony" perhaps for the last time. But if he was not to be present for this ritual next season others would be, for the fish were returning and his people would eat this winter. That was enough.[1]

CHAPTER **2**

The Salmon People

The people of the North Pacific Coast were, and still are "The Salmon People". Though there was infinite variety in form, some sort of rite similar to the one just related usually marked the arrival of the first salmon to be caught as the annual migration headed up the rivers and streams to spawn.

The first fish was treated as an honoured guest of the rank of a visiting chief. They believed that the salmon permitted itself to be harpooned or clubbed, or captured in certain definite ways consistent with the practice of the local tribe and family unit, but it was extremely bad luck to molest a fish in any other way. Many tribes told a story to their children describing the terrible fate that befell a naughty boy who poked out the eyes of a salmon. Since the salmon's soul was immortal, a mistreated one might warn the others not to return to a certain stream, thus bringing tragedy to the people who had misused the privilege of eating their flesh. To the aboriginals of Canada's west coast it was imperative that the life-giver be treated with respect. The Salmon People fitted into the total scheme of things.

To the south of the Tsimshians were the Kwakiutls, famous for their almost complete ritualization of life. They too marked the capture of the first salmon. Apart from the general ceremonies, of which there were several, every good Kwakiutl fisherman had his own prayers which belonged to him personally and which he addressed to his first salmon of the season:

"Swimmer, I thank you because I am still alive at this season when you come back to our good place, for the reason why you come is that we may play together with my fishing tackle, Swimmer. Now, go home and tell your friends that you had good luck on account of your coming here and that they shall come with their wealth, that I may get some of your wealth, Swimmer. Also take away my sickness friend, supernatural one, Swimmer."[1]

For these people life depended upon the fish. The dense coniferous forests clinging to the cheeks of the mountains were infested with a variety of small deer and on the craggy summits stout goats could be hunted for their meat, hair and horns. But the terrain made hunting difficult, travel almost impossible, and there was no large game such as the caribou or the buffalo of the plains (though a stunted cousin of the caribou once did exist on the Queen Charlotte Islands). Indeed, it is a wonder that people would settle in this dull, forbidding land of few gentle beaches or flat lands, where soil is shallow and sour, where the warm vapour of the Japanese current blots out the sun for weeks at a time and it rains relentlessly. Yet for countless generations a large aboriginal population found not only sustenance here, but time to develop an astonishingly high level of culture. The reason for this was the salmon.

Every year the phenomenal runs swept in from the ocean and surged up the streams and rivers to spawn. From Alaska to California, wave upon wave, they came by the millions, strong, graceful, swift and bold. Huge silver-sided springs, powerfully built, fierce feeders on herring and needle-fish, growing to an average weight of twenty-five pounds; wary seven-pound sockeye that feed almost entirely on shrimps and other tiny hard-shelled creatures; the smaller hump-backs, so called because of the grotesque shape they develop upon approaching and entering the rivers; the strong, shining cohoe, a magnificent jumper and a bold navigator of small streams; and the ferocious chum or dog-salmon with its hooked nose and huge fangs that develop in its

later life — these are the five species of salmon which for countless generations invaded the west coast to bring life to the raven-
haired people who lived there.

They were coming when the first white man plied the placid
waters of the coastal fjords and inlets. They were coming in
as far back as the memory of the masked dances, the songs and
the stories of the ingenious people whose ancestors crossed from
Asia on the Aleutian land bridge to settle in this formidable
region of mountain peaks, innumerable islands and long, lonely
inlets.

The fish fed these people of the coast. They fed their relatives
who settled far inland along the banks of the Nass, the Skeena,
the Fraser and their tributaries, for salmon return to spawn at
the gravel beds where they themselves were spawned high up
in the mountains at the sources of the streams that feed these
great rivers. When in 1808 Simon Fraser, with his intrepid voya-
geurs, made his way down the river that bears his name, he lived
on salmon dried and baled the previous year. Only the tall trees
and tumbling rocks knew for sure how long the Indians had been
catching salmon with their dip-nets at the ancestral fishing places
along the banks.

The same could be said of the Skeena and its tributaries far
to the north. Where the Bulkley joins the Skeena at the site of the
present town of Hazelton, under the brow of Roche de Boule and
175 miles from the mouth of the misty river, the people caught
salmon. Still further north through the wild valley gashed in
the mountains by the angry river, the Babine joins the Skeena.
Here, too, there lived a people who depended upon the coming
of the fish.

In 1904 a fishery inspector made a trip through this land of
treacherous beauty. At one spot on the Babine River he discovered some sixteen houses, thirty feet by twenty-seven feet
and eight feet high, filled with tiers of salmon being smoked.
Besides this on both banks were acres of racks loaded with fish-
flesh drying in the sun. An Indian family used approximately
1,000 sockeye salmon every winter, and the inspector estimated

10

that close to three-quarters of a million fish were being caught at the two barricades he encountered. What he discovered had in all probability been going on uninterrupted for hundreds of years until the coming of the white man.

On the Thompson River, the major tributary of the Fraser, there is archeological evidence of a very ancient population with settlements straggling along the banks adjacent to the main supply of food and wealth. But the most startling evidence of the long-standing relationship of the people to the fish is found right in the Fraser Canyon. Here in 1960 a group of archeologists dug to a depth of twenty-five feet, five inches. At various levels they discovered charred pits of wild cherries, the oldest of which reported an age of close to 9,000 years. Wild cherries ripen precisely at the time of year when the salmon pass up the river to spawn and when the Indians would naturally catch them in great numbers. So, seven thousand years before the disciples of Jesus fished the Sea of Galilee, it may be surmised, when the high water level of the Fraser was sixty feet above the mean high water mark now, people sat by their camp fires watching splayed carcasses of salmon toast before the flames, spitting wild cherry stones into the ashes.[2]

Some of the catch taken at these ancestral fishing spots would travel hundreds of miles and pass through many hands before it found its way into the feasting bowl. Properly dried and smoked it could be kept in the storehouse for up to two years if turned over in the sun after the first year. Salmon dried, pounded and baled as pemmican, was used as currency for bartering in the vigorous trade that was carried on between the tribes. It was only a twelve mile pack by Eagle Pass from the fisheries at Three Valley Lake to the Columbia opposite where the town of Revelstoke now stands. From there little effort was required to take preserved salmon by canoe through the great region stretching to the south.

Preserving was an art which the people had developed to a fine degree. First the salmon was dried in the sun or in houses. Then it was pounded into shreds between two stones and packed

11

tightly into baskets made of grass, rushes or cedar strips (depending on the locality). The baskets, which might be two feet long and one foot in diameter, were lined with salmon skins dried and stretched as waterproofing. When they were filled and sealed with more skins they weighed close to one hundred pounds. For storing, seven of these bales were stood together in a dry place out of reach of wolves and other hungry denizens of the forest. Another five were placed on top. Then the whole mound was covered with woven mats and secured with thongs.

Fish prepared in this way would keep for years, or might be transported many miles. For example, salmon purchased or won at the game of SLIK-A-MIOUS in the Shuswap country, after reaching where Colville now stands would be lost at TS-LALIKUM (Okanagan for the identical game) to Indians from farther south.

The fish determined where the people lived. No accurate figure can be given, but intelligent estimates of the aboriginal population of what is now British Columbia are set at approximately 80,000, an impressively high population density for native North America, and about forty percent of the total native population of all Canada. The obvious reason for this concentration of people was the availability of food and that food was salmon. In the interior the people lived close to the rivers because they were highways through the forests as well as conveyors upon which their protein arrived. A population map would show the areas about the main salmon rivers shaded dark. Rivers which consistently failed to breed salmon were not populated.

Up on the Nass that cuts its way through the teeming forests and past the snow-packed peaks of Alaska to enter the ocean just below the Panhandle, the village of the Niska people huddled close to the banks. On the upper Skeena were the people of the Gitksan dialect, while the main body of Tsimshians controlled the valuable Skeena area from its broad, muddy mouth back through the valley with its shimmering poplars and birches, on through the roaring canyon that in later years would tax the boilers of the sternwheelers owned by Cunningham and Hudson's Bay

Company — on up to the Seven Sisters Peaks who are really beautiful maidens frozen into rock because their hearts were as hard as stone when being wooed by seven young warriors disguised as beavers many moons ago. The names of the villages in this region, to this day, can be pronounced properly only by the people themselves or by the crafty ravens who sit with tilted heads upon the topmost branches of the cedars — Kitsumkalum, Kitwanga, Kwinitsa.

Carrier Indians clustered about the Bulkley and the Babine, which flow north into the Skeena, as well as around the "big bend" of the Fraser and the Stuart and Nechako rivers which join the Fraser where Prince George now stands. A few people lived on the banks of the Salmon River further north.

There were Indians of the Carrier band about Takla and Stuart lakes and on the other great sockeye salmon spawning lakes to the south of these — Francois and Fraser. These lakes were among the major spawning grounds of the Fraser system, yet in spite of this the Indians who lived upon them were poorly located and their numbers were not concentrated, for by the time the salmon reached here they were not only fewer in numbers, having been fished by people further downstream and having been culled by the eliminating processes of nature, but they were poor specimens compared to the bright, vigorous hoards which had entered the river as much as two-and-a-half months earlier. They had been battered against the sharp rocks of the canyon and tossed by the turbulent water of Hell's Gate — a name that was to become connected with their near extinction. Their bodies were emaciated, for salmon do not eat once they approach fresh water. When caught their stomachs are almost always empty and indeed relatively free of living bacteria. By the time they reach the spawning beds the once graceful fish are deformed out of all recognition. Their bodies have turned a bright crimson so that during large runs the water looks as though it were streaked with blood. White spots of fungus may already be appearing on the flanks and head. The snout of the male is elongated and vicious looking, for he must fight off intruding males while waiting for his

13

mate to dig the redd in which to lay her eggs, and once the eggs are laid and fertilized both male and female are exhausted and their wasted carcases are strewn for miles along the banks. In such condition they did not provide the appetizing meat enjoyed by the various Interior Salish bands to the south, nor did they compare with the strong, full-bodied fish caught in salt water.

Nevertheless, these interior people waited patiently each year as did the Chilcotins and the Shuswaps further south, for by late summer their provisions from the previous year were depleted and the days were eked out cautiously upon scraps of woodlike dried fish, while the men kept a watchful eye upon the pools and eddies. Early in the spring and summer they might catch a few spring salmon which would be a welcome treat after the dry diet of winter, and now and then a gigantic sturgeon could be landed that would feed the whole village. But the illustrious sockeye was the main staple, and often the spawners arrived just in time to save the people from starvation, or at least from the humility of having to go to a neighbouring tribe to beg for food. When the white man came for fur, he too found himself anxiously waiting with the natives for food which on any one particular stream might or might not come.

Daniel W. Harmon, a trader with the North West Fur Company, was at Stuart Lake in 1811. By August 2nd of that year a grim situation existed at the little outpost trading station. Harmon wrote in his diary:

"Our whole stock of provisions in the fort for ten persons consists of five salmon only. It is impossible at this season to take fish out of this lake or river. Unless the salmon from the sea soon make their appearance our condition will be deplorable."[3]

There were tense days as the last five dried salmon were rationed out among the men, for the people who brought fur and fish to the fort now brought stories of starvation and hunger, of long tortuous trips down river to trade with those closer to the "stinking lake" who had salmon to spare. But by Thursday, August 22nd, the tension broke and Harmon went to his diary in a better mood than he had enjoyed for some weeks.

14

"One of the Natives has caught a salmon which is joyful intelligence to us all, for we hope and expect that in a few days we shall have them in abundance."

He went on to note,

"These fish visit, to a greater or less extent, all the rivers in this region, and form the principal dependence of the inhabitants as a means of subsistence."[4]

Even here, hidden from the ocean by 700 miles of mountains, these little bands of native people looked to the salmon for survival. Their lot was precarious for not every stream, not every spawning-bed yielded abundance each year, and where a family clan relied upon the products of a particular fishing place the winter was dreaded if the fish had not arrived in numbers by late summer or early fall. Whenever they did arrive it was cause for celebration. In 1812 Harmon wrote:

"Salmon begin to come up this river. As soon as one is caught the natives always make a feast to express their joy at the arrival of these fish. The person who first sees a salmon in the river exclaims, TA LOE NAS LAY, TA LOE NAS LAY, in English, 'Salmon have arrived, Salmon have arrived', and the exclamation is caught with joy and uttered with animation by every person in the village."[5]

Yet it was on the coast and about the lower reaches of the Fraser, more than anywhere else, that the inhabitants were truly the "Salmon People". The tall Haida warriors of the Queen Charlottes enjoyed the lively, late summer runs that entered their streams. The Tsimshians clustered about the Nass and the Skeena Rivers. The Kwakiutls dominated the central coast region and the northern portion of Vancouver Island. Before the white man came with his technical advantages there were more Nootka Indians living on the wind-swept coast of Vancouver Island than there are Indians and whites today, for in those days there were fish to support the population.

But the main concentration was in the south. Great numbers of Halkomelems of the Coast Salish linguist group lived about the southeastern corner of Vancouver Island where the gigantic runs of sockeye swept through the straits of Juan de Fuca. About the mouth of the Fraser River and along its lower banks lived

15

the Halkomelems of the Coast Salish nation, although they were in no way able to exercise a monopoly over this, the most prolific sockeye river in the world.

In July, August and September, the Fraser was visited by thousands of Indians. They came in canoes with their families. They came by the hundreds in war canoes fifty feet in length and six or seven feet in the beam, the bows with intricate carving rising high out of the water. They formed barges by lashing planks between canoes ten to twelve feet apart and sailed up the murky waterway to below the first rapids where the salmon could be scooped out with long, slender dip-nets or speared with deft jabs of the harpoon. Thousands made their way up to the rapids. Where the sides were steep they fished from flimsy platforms protruding from the banks or from rock causeways built out into the swift water.

Those from the coast met and often clashed with the tribes who considered this annual visit an encroachment, for the upper banks of the Fraser were strewn with villages, each one claiming exclusive rights to fish at given points. There was excitement and confusion when the fish were running. There was fighting and bloodshed and though they usually left serious skirmishes till after the fish had passed an old insult would be remembered once the winter food supply was secured. The Fort Langley Journal entry for Friday, October 19, 1827, tells of a war party of "Chowitchens" coming back down from the fishery with the head of a victim impaled as a pendant on the bow stem of their canoe.

Life on the coast was not utopian, but the salmon people were proud masters of their art. There was never a shortage of food on the coast, as there often was in the interior, so that these people who captured their supplies with dip-net and harpoon, stone weir and cedar basket traps during a few months of the year, were able to devote time to the development and preservation of their art and culture. They were superior to the "stick" Indians, as they called them, simply because they had a superior larder. Wherever there were fish there were people, and with

16

incredible regularity the waters of the inlets and bays, the rivers and lakes yielded the silver harvest, and the people ate and lived.

All of this was to change for the salmon people. For countless generations they had fished for food and for purposes of bartering among themselves. Then came the white man and the quiet world of the coast was smashed with the clanking of machinery and the explosion of guns. Now the Indians learned to fish and trap, not for food and clothing, but for trinkets and whisky. Now they had to fish for themselves *and* for the white man. Then came other white men and the long, lonely inlets were disfigured by the erection of canneries that belched fumes into the low-lying clouds and spewed waste into the tide, and the Indian learned to fish for the white man's hungry machines.

Today in the villages and fish camps scattered from Vancouver to Prince Rupert there are many wizened old Indians who remember with nostalgia the days when there were lots of fish for their people, days that are gone now.

17

CHAPTER **3**

Fish and Fur

No one knows for sure how long the copper skinned people of the coast enjoyed the monopoly they held over its silvery riches. No one knows for sure how long the dramatic migration of fish had been coming on its relentless return to the spawning grounds. Change touched lightly upon this wild world of rocks and rushing seas. The forests and watery valleys knew only the sound of ravens croaking, the plaintive cry of seagulls wheeling in the wind. Seals and sea lions pursued the myriads of salmon and behind them came whales lancing the surface with their broad fins, dusting the horizon with their spray. Perhaps a dull, monotonous chunk! chunk! could be heard resounding from the beach, back through the bush, as a cedar log yielded to the stone adze. Then, quite ruthlessly change marched in upon this world, marring and maiming it forever.

Fur receives a great amount of attention in most annals of the conquest of the West Coast. It is usually pointed out that though the explorers failed to find the north-west passage, they discovered a source of wealth far greater than anything anticipated by the treasure-seekers of the seas — namely furs which were by this time in fashionable demand back in Europe. What is seldom, if ever, recognized is that the primary riches of the coast was not fur but fish, for without the runs of salmon this formidable frontier would have supported very little life, animal or human. The fish fed the mink, the seal and otter. Fish fed the men who trapped these fur-bearers. And when the white man came trading over the gunwale with knives and nails, beads and buttons, and more devastating, guns and whisky, fresh salmon from the natives was a welcome relief after months of salt pork. A beach seine-net soon came to be included as an indispensable piece of equipment on voyages to the Pacific Coast, for with it, at the proper season, hundreds of salmon could be caught in one scoop.

When Captain George Vancouver came out from England following the "Nootka Difficulty" in 1795 to officially reclaim the territory from the Spanish he completely missed the Columbia River and the Fraser, a costly misfortune for the British. However, he did come through the straits of Juan de Fuca and was the first to circumnavigate the island that now bears his name. It was June of the year, the time when the early runs of sockeye were jumping in the bays, and all along the coast from Burrard Inlet north, Vancouver and his men met the Indians at their fishing places and traded with them for supplies of the succulent salmon. In Burrard Inlet they traded trinkets for great quantities of fresh fish. Further north at Jervis Inlet they did the same. In Deep Bay they were astounded by the immensity of the fish stages that stood along the shore, ingeniously lashed together by withes of pine root. At Cape Mudge they noted the Indian nets hanging on stakes outside the houses.

On through the treacherous waters of Johnstone Straits and Seymour Narrows this ex-midshipman of Captain Cook sailed the *Discovery,* rounded Cape Scott, slid down the west coast of the island and entered Nootka Sound where he met Quadra and made arrangements to supervise the evacuation of the Spanish garrison from their sixteen-gun fortress on the small island at the entrance of Friendly Cove. And all along the way he and his men enjoyed the rich, red meat of the sockeye.

Following this, a growing number of vessels manned by adventuresome and sometimes barbarous traders, rounded the Horn and sailed into the sullen skies of the northwest in search of furs.

19

A steady stream of pelts began to flow from the interior down to the coast to help meet the demand, but little did these economic adventurers realize that the swarms of salmon which darted away from their hulls would provide a much longer lasting, and eventually a more abundant source of revenue than the highly prized pelts.

By the early part of the nineteenth century, except for the war years of 1812-14, this coastal trade was dominated by American ships sailing out of Boston. In 1824 George Simpson, the governor of the northern department of Hudson's Bay Company, arrived at Fort George (Fort Astoria) near the mouth of the Columbia River. He was just British enough to determine to outdo the Americans in this coastal commerce, though Scotch enough to be alarmed at the extravagance of the men in the company's western posts. They would have to develop a taste for salmon and do with less imported goods so that the trade vessels could carry more articles for barter. Besides, the future of the Columbia River district did not look bright for the Hudson's Bay Company due to growing tension over the lack of a western boundary. Consequently a reconnaissance party set out from Fort George in November of that year to scan the territory around Fraser's River and Burrard Inlet for a likely fort location.

James McMillan was picked for the job. He was a staunch Scot with a build like a block of granite and a will as strong as oak — just the right sort of man to head such an expedition. With a party of forty men, some of whom were Sandwich Islanders and Iroquois, he portaged and paddled, swatted and swore his way to Puget Sound, up the eastern channel into Boundary Bay, where they entered the Nicomekl River, followed it as far as possible, slushed through the damp, black soil of Langley Prairie pounded by rains till they found Salmon River and descended it to the Fraser itself; and in spite of all this brought back a glowing report of the possibilities for prosperity on the Fraser.

Three years later, McMillan found himself camped with twenty-five men opposite the south end of Whidbey Island, purchasing salmon to eat from Washkaladga and Sinoktin, two old chiefs who each received a few beads, a little tobacco and a looking-glass for their produce. McMillan and his men were waiting for the schooner, *Cadboro* which picked them up July 12th. It took three days to reach the mouth of the Fraser, then nine days to find a channel through the sand-heads. Finally they entered the river and continued upstream — when there was wind enough to drive them against the stiff current — past the place which McMillan had marked with an HB on a tree three years earlier.

When they dropped anchor one of the first acts of the crew was to buy salmon from the natives. It was almost a symbolic act, for though they had come this far intending to corner the fur market, it was the fish which would keep Fort Langley alive after her usefulness as a fur trading station had declined. Fort Langley was the first real settlement west of the Canadian Rockies. Its establishment marked another stage in the advance of change upon the hitherto quiet land of the salmon people.

Life within the first crude fort was a mixture of hard work, strict discipline, unexpected mishaps and occasional measures of rum. Archibald McDonald, who shortly took over from McMillan, was harassed with problems that ranged from a case of syphilis among his men to placating the temperamental natives.

Salmon runs were extremely poor in the early fall of 1828 and it was difficult to procure enough from the Indians, many of whom had already left the fishing places above the fort to get what they could at other streams. By September 27th they had only about five thousand pieces of dried salmon and ten barrels salted; not nearly enough to keep the fort going all winter, for the daily ration was four fish per man, and the annual consumption at a post came to about twenty-five thousand fish.

Indeed, about one-third of the Hudson's Bay Company's annual expense in western trade went for purchasing salmon and other fish from the Indians, or paying them for their services as fishermen. The Rev. Father Morice, who spent many years in the interior, estimated that by 1836 the fur posts of New Caledonia were consuming an average of 67,510 salmon annually.

21

If salmon was scarce the Indian and the trader alike went hungry, though once again it was the interior forts as well as the interior Indians who suffered most, for they normally relied upon one run of fish. If that run failed they were in distress.

The plight of the Indians was pathetic in such circumstances. Before the white man came they knew that it was absolutely imperative to store enough dried fish for winter. If the run failed on their own river there was quite often an agreement with a neighbouring tribe whereby they could fish in that tribe's territory. When salmon failed among the Chilcotins, for example, they were always permitted by the Indians further down the Fraser, to fish for food on the Fraser itself. But with the coming of the white man the Indian learned to depend upon the trading post for food and goods. He traded his fish for tobacco, vermillion rings and other trash, then in the dead of winter he trudged through the snow to the door of the trading post willing to give even the highly prized beaver pelt for salmon which he had supplied earlier in the season, but which by now the fort could not afford to let go.

Often the chief trader was obliged to send dog-sleds to a distant fort for loads of dried fish in order to keep alive the members of his post as well as the wretched Indians upon whose trapping and fishing the whole business largely depended. In 1827, the year in which Fort Langley was built, an interior trader reported that the Indians from Kamloops to Fort St. James were so scantily fed that they could not be employed in any hard labour.[1] Many died of starvation.

The situation was never this critical at Langley. Still, McDonald had ambitions for the resource that swam past the palisades and he was more than relieved when in October, the month he actually took over, salmon became more plentiful. He put five men and several of the wives to work all day cleaning, salting and smoking the piles of fish brought by the Indians, who by this time had their own winter supplies well secured.

It was one thing to procure fish, another thing to preserve it properly. No matter how they kept fires going in the fish shed, no matter how often they rubbed it, mould formed on the slender slices of dried flesh because of the damp atmosphere. Finally, in desperation, McDonald, like his predecessor, resorted to storing the fish in the men's houses. There it was — thousands of carcases hanging from the beams and rafters, filling the quarters with a pungent odour surpassed only by the acid scent of wet buck-skins and the stench of bodies.

There was one way to alleviate this problem of preserving, that was to salt the fish in barrels or tierces. But here again McDonald ran into difficulties, for there was no one at the post proficient enough in the tricky art of cooperage to build barrels that would keep the fish for any length of time. In spite of repeated pleas sent to Governor George Simpson for a cooper, they were forced for several years to improvise with crude casks made by men whose skills were as meagre as their hopes were great.

Salt, an essential ingredient in the curing, was hard to get and initially the authorities were not at all pleased with the idea of sending the quantities Archibald McDonald ordered. Simpson's theory was to have the ships carry only the bare necessities for the forts — the rest of the cargo to be articles for bartering. In spite of continual frustration, McDonald and his group of ten men and one clerk managed to put down over two hundred barrels of salmon in the summer of 1830, some of which were sent to Dr. John McLaughlin, Chief Factor at Fort Vancouver, in the hope that they might be worthy of export.

The result was disappointing. Many of the barrels "lost their pickle" and the fish had to be eaten before going bad. It was doubtful in fact, whether fish done in this way could be expected to make the long trip through severe climatic fluctuations around The Horn and twice across the equator to England.

But McDonald was resolute. He could not think of the tremendous wealth of the fisheries going unexploited. True, there were lean years. But other seasons, from bank to bank the murky water of the river leapt with life. So thick were the sockeye in good years that early traders were afraid to enter the river lest their boats be capsized by the surging schools. Far out on the Pacific the water danced with flashes of silver as the mighty hoards pressed on, driven by an inexplicable instinct to seek the very stream where they had been hatched four years earlier. Through the Juan de Fuca straits they came, wave upon wave, on through Puget Sound meeting and mingling with thousands of other fish which had slipped down through Johnstone Straits and the Straits of Georgia. Here and there small runs broke off from the migration, instinctively recognizing their home river, while the main body moved inexorably to where the gaping mouth of the Fraser, like some mythological serpent, waited to devour them.

Langley stood on the south bank some thirty-five miles from the mouth, and at a spot where an arm of the river crooked around two islands. It was a pugnacious little ensemble of not-so-solid timber pitted against a world of overwhelming wildness. Outside the 135 foot by 120 foot palisaded enclosure, McDonald had thirty bushels of potatoes planted, the first farming in the valley, and from the four foot gallery the men could look down on the river and watch the Indians driving their canoes with steady stroke up to the fisheries. Underneath their cedar hulls, splashing on every side were the salmon, wild and wary, but in such incredible abundance that there were times when it was impossible to paddle without striking their slippery sides.

No matter what preparations were made at the fort, they could not handle all the fish brought by the Indians once the main runs began each summer. A thousand bright sockeye, and more, were often traded before eight o'clock in the morning, and though it saddened McDonald and frustrated and bewildered the Indians, forty to fifty canoes each loaded with at least that number of fish were often turned away.

Eventually a cooper was sent from England and the drab days of winter rang with the echo of creaking staves and hammered hoops, while the stack of barrels grew higher — well-made barrels that were filled with layers of salt and fillets and

24

shipped to the Hawaiian Islands in the Fall. Thus began New Caledonia's export trade.

In 1833 Archibald McDonald was succeeded by a hard-headed little man called James Murray Yale, who along with this rudimentary industry inherited all the perplexities of over-seeing the fort. By 1839 the poorly constructed fort that had been hurriedly whacked together under the vigilance of the *Cadboro* was showing unabashed signs of dilapidation.

The decline in furs had jeopardized Langley's existence, but Dr. McLaughlin — known to the Indians as "Great White Eagle" on account of his long, white locks — was instrumental in saving the fort because of the growing salmon industry. It was decided to rebuild Langley two miles upstream on the same bank.

Yale threw himself into the task with characteristic energy and before long a new, larger Langley stood on the brow of a ridge overlooking the winding river. Within less than a year however, he and his men were living in a cluster of tents beside a heap of smouldering ashes; all their work in vain. A few days later the tall stack of the *Beaver* — the first steamboat on the coast — swerved into view amidstream, and the work of construction was recommenced, this time under the leadership of a rather ill-tempered "Little Yale" who told Chief Factor Douglas, who had come on an official visit, to leave six good axes and be off out of the way. By next season Fort Langley was in business as usual.

Gradually the shipments of salt salmon increased. In spite of the disastrous fire of 1840 four hundred barrels were prepared for export to Hawaii that season. About twenty-five miles upstream, close to the Indian fishing places, a saltery was established, which in spite of being burned and rebuilt in the middle of the 1848 season, still managed to ship out seventeen hundred barrels of salt salmon — barrels that would fetch as high as £2:10 each in Hawaii.

The whole character of the coast was changing as the veil of isolation was rent, cleaved by the coming of white men eager to grab and be gone, but more so by those willing to come and stay.

By the time the Oregon Treaty of 1846 put an end to the belligerent "54-40 or fight" slogan of the Yankees, Victoria, which had been established as a fort just three years before, was nothing more than a sprawling pile of posts and palisades adjoined by a few acres of cultivated land.

In spite of the boundary settlement there was apprehension in the minds of many a home government official as to the ultimate fate of Vancouver Island if it were not soon settled with loyal British subjects. One fort could not hope to hold the island if American settlers began to move in. Consequently on January 13, 1849, subject to the payment of seven shillings annually and the promise to settle resident colonists from Great Britain and Ireland or other parts of the Dominion, Hudson's Bay Company was granted the territory of Vancouver Island, and a couple of years later — after one abortive attempt at settlement at Sooke — the first load of permanent residents arrived on the boat *Tory*. They had been six months and two weeks on the voyage.

Now with an expanding population the fish were in greater demand and the Hudson's Bay Company was eager to meet the need for food with increased fishing. Consequently on the first of May in the same year that saw the arrival of the settlers, William John McDonald arrived in Victoria from his native Isle of Skye, and was immediately sent to the San Juan Islands along with three or four French Canadians to cure salmon. They built a log cabin and shed and spent three summers there purchasing salmon from the natives at the rate of sixty for a four-dollar blanket.

Victoria continued to grow. On Sunday morning April 25, 1858, the town people were surprised as they came out of church to see an American wooden side-wheeler sliding in to the landing, her decks choked with red, flannel-shirted miners. The *Commodore* brought the first load of knife and revolver-toting bonanza seekers who used Victoria as a jumping off place for the Fraser. Many of that first load of 450 foundered attempting to cross the sound in canoes or rafts. But the rush was on and nothing could stop it now. Before the year was out some 25,000 men had sailed up the Fraser in search of gold. Some found it!

The tidal wave of humanity receded before long, dragging with it disillusionment if not pokes of gold dust. But pools of population were left behind, and the character of the country was irreversibly changed. The Hudson's Bay Company monopoly was broken, settlement was spreading, farming expanded and trade bristled.

Gone were the quiet days. Gone were the days when traders could purchase fish with a few buttons, when a blanket would fetch a canoe-load full. Now the great schools of salmon, which for countless centuries had survived against the vicissitudes of nature and the persistent but economical fishing of the Indians —were to be subjected to the tactics of money-makers who plundered the stocks with little regard for the future, not necessarily because they did not care about the future (though obviously many did not) but because they believed the fantastic runs to be inexhaustible. The fish now faced their greatest enemy: the white man and his industry.

CHAPTER **4**

Canning Comes
to the Coast

When William Hume came to California in the spring of 1852 he had little more than the net which he had made back in his home town of Augusta, Maine, where he and his father had fished in the Kennebec River, and where his father and grand-father had been in the business from as early as 1780. Indeed, his ancestors had fished the sportive salmon of the Tweed and Tay in Scotland for generations.

In 1849 gold dust from mining-mad California reached Boston, in a used Underwood can, and thousands of men poured into the west, hot with the fever of gold in their veins, lured on by the magic of Marshall's discovery on the little stream that emerged from the Sierra Nevada mountains about half a day's journey from Sutter's Fort. But while thousands gouged the river beds and scratched the faces of the hills in search of gold, William Hume threw his net into the Sacramento River and found a fortune in silver — the silver of the thrashing salmon which he sold to the miners and prospectors.

After four years he went back to Maine for a visit. His tales of the incredible runs of huge Quinnat salmon caught the imagination of his three younger brothers, George, Robert and Joseph, so they returned to Sacramento with him and began work on the little cabin which William had purchased at the foot of K street, right on the bank of the river. By 1864, when the nation was in the throes of civil war, a boyhood pal of George Hume by the name of Andrew Hapgood, a tinsmith by trade, joined the Humes and immediately went to work preparing tins for what was to be the first commercial salmon cannery on the west coast.

Preserving any kind of food stuffs in cans was at this time an industry in its early infancy. In fact the whole thing had got started just sixty years before, during the Napoleonic wars.

Napoleon Bonaparte had trouble feeding his armies. The pesky English Navy kept blockading his ports, and it was almost impossible to keep hardtack, smoked fish and salt meat from mildewing and decaying before it reached his far-flung battalions. In desperation he announced a prize of twelve-hundred francs for the man who would invent some method of preserving food that would reach his armies in safe, edible nourishing condition.

The prize was won by Nicolas Appert, an erstwhile chef, pickler and preserver, wine-maker and brewer, confectioner and distiller, who for over a dozen years had been experimenting in his steamy little shop, placing different foods in wide-mouthed jars, fastening the corks with wire and boiling them for various lengths of time. It was in the year 1809, half a century before his countryman, Pasteur, coupled disease, and incidentally food decay, with bacteria, that Nicolas Appert gave the world: "The Art of Preserving Animal and Vegetable Substances for Many Years".[1]

Nicolas Appert learned to his financial sorrow that boiling water was not always hot enough to stop spoiling. Even after the English chemist, Sir Humphrey Davy had experimentally raised the boiling point of water to 240 degrees by adding calcium chloride, losses were heavy and frequent in those primitive days of preserving, and the glass jars were vulnerable to breakage as well as heavy in shipping. But the ground work was laid and while progress was not rapid to begin, it was inevitable.

By 1815, having capitalized on Peter Durant's invention of a tin canister, Appert was packing and selling food sealed in tinplate, a process which many were convinced would be the ruination of the human race. In spite of some general skepticism there was something of a stampede into the new industry, one that was to revolutionize the eating habits of the human race, which was to have far-reaching social and economic implications and which made such a devastating impact upon the lives of the coastal people and the existence of the salmon runs. In Canada Tristam Halliday built what was the first salmon cannery in the North American Continent on the Bay of Fundy in the year 1840. But it was Hapgood and Hume who brought canning to the west coast.

In their little shed at the foot of K street the work was laborious. Methods were still primitive, painfully slow since each can had to be hand-made, and precarious in success. Nevertheless the Hapgood-Hume team was determined. They divided the work. William Hume was a ruddy outdoors type who loved the feel of rain in his face and the smart of oars in his hardened hands. He did the fishing. George looked after the office while Robert tended the tinsmithing along with Andrew Hapgood. Young Joseph was general factotum.

For months before the season opened the little charcoal pots glowed, keeping the soldering irons hot beside the stacks of pencil solder and the jars of muriatic acid. Ends were snipped with shears then stamped by a hand press. Sides were cut, then shaped on the reamer. Methodically the tinsmith ran the soldering iron up the seam and around the end of each individual can. A hundred a day could be made ready if he were industrious. But in spite of this tedious process, at the end of the 1864 season the firm of Hapgood and Hume had cooked some 2,000 cases of canned salmon in the windowless cooking room where only Andrew Hapgood was allowed to enter lest the secret formula be discovered.

At around $20.00 per case in England there was a handsome profit from the first shipment, and even though the following year saw a drop in price to approximately $16.00 Hapgood and Hume had learned from their experience. With improved methods and a larger pack profits were again high. The salmon canning industry was launched.

Mention the California gold rush — or any of the western gold rushes for that matter — and the imagination of every adventure-lover is jerked into activity. But equally spectacular and exciting, and greater in monetary returns, though seldom mentioned, was the "salmon rush". Money-hungry men whose appetites had already been whetted in the goldfields, charged into the business eager to make the rapid fortune that had eluded them, or to expand the stake they had managed to carry out of the mines. There were bonanzas for fishermen and canners alike, but as in the gold rush there were casualties and dismal failures. The greatest tragedy however, was what happened to the fish.

As the number of canneries and fishermen increased the fish decreased. The runs were decimated in the frenzy to land as many as possible, and by the indiscriminate waste of fly-by-night canners. But more devastating by far was the hydraulic mining back in the mountains where tons of gravel and earth were flushed away to get at the gold. Acres of splendid spawning beds were smothered under mud, or washed away completely.

Early travellers through the territory around the upper reaches of the Sacramento used to be awed by the myriads of salmon that choked the river on their final phase of life before spawning. Those that had already spawned and spent themselves were flung up on the banks in thousands. The ravens picked out their eyes. Bears licked the putrid flesh from the bones, and the air was heavy with the acrid stench for miles around — but their eggs were safely stored under eighteen inches of clean gravel and in the spring the inch long alevins would wiggle to life: another generation would be born.

Then, within the space of a few years hydraulic mining and avaricious fishing reduced the Sacramento runs to a negligible number of stragglers who fought the futile battle for survival, spending their ultimate ounce of energy to reach the spawning beds, only to discover thick mud where there should be gravel.

Pale, orange-pink eggs leaked from their exhausted bodies

31

and were gobbled down by waiting trout. The next generation of salmon from that stream would depend upon the few females fortunate enough to find a favourable place to deposit their eggs, and lucky enough to be accompanied by a male to squirt the spawn with his fertilizing milt. Soon commercial fishing was a hopeless venture on the Sacramento River.

The same fate befell the Columbia River runs. Then, when the Americans had impoverished their own fish resources they turned to Canadian supplies and commenced to ruin them.

William Hume anticipated this decline in the Sacramento stocks. Besides, it was in keeping with his pioneering spirit to seek a domain away from the growing jostle of the city. He headed north, carved a clearing in the bush near the mouth of the Columbia River, built a house and cannery, and apart from occasional winters spent in San Francisco, he lived there for the next forty years.

In San Francisco he would be seen dressed immaculately in cut-away suit, bow-tie, white starched shirt with a diamond pin, high silk hat and brown kid gloves. He was a dandy on the side-walks of the city. But his heart was in the bush. In early spring, upon returning to the cannery he would hurry past the men like one with an urgent mission, go directly to the house and change into his doeskin trousers, blue flannel shirt and high-laced boots. Then he would emerge with a relaxed smile and move among his men, shaking hands.

Robert Hume bought up twenty miles of frontage on the Rogue River and became known as "The King of Rogue River". George, who liked the city life, moved over into fruit canning and amassed a fortune at it. Young Joseph did not enjoy the conspicuous success of his older brothers, but he shared in the fame of the Humes, who along with Andrew Hapgood get credit for pioneering salmon canning on the west coast.

Once the coast of California and Washington were exploited it was just a step to the Fraser.

CHAPTER **5**

On to the Fraser

James Syme was on every count a remarkable man. Born in Edinburgh, Scotland, he pulled up roots at the age of twenty-seven and came to San Francisco where for the next three years, although he was actually an architect, he made a success of ornamental plastering and modelling. He was a sensitive man by nature, a gifted oil-painter whose displayed works showed a vigorous style that may have been in compensation for his not-too-robust constitution. By all appearances he was anything but the pioneering type. In 1862 amid the motley crews of hard-bitten prospectors and miners who roamed the Cariboo Country in the skirmish for gold, James Syme could be found doggedly keeping up with the rest, whether knee-deep in paralyzing water or trudging the tortuous trails.

When he moved down to New Westminster in the spring of 1867 prospects looked good for a while. He had a little money saved from his diggings and a clear idea how to invest it. Canning had not yet reached the Fraser. It was an open field. Someone with imagination and energy could make a fortune by being first to can salmon on the Fraser River, and James Syme was determined to be that person.

According to initial indications he ought to have succeeded, for samples of his two pound tins of Fraser River sockeye, which he had cooked on the kitchen stove, were exhibited at the

Agricultural Show in New Westminster in October 1867, and the product was given special mention for its quality. Already he was shipping cured salmon and oolichans[1] to the mining camps in the Cariboo, and the few cans of cooked salmon he had sent were well received. But he knew that a larger more reliable market had to be discovered, so when Captain Alex Barrack sailed to Australia that fall, besides a shipment of salted salmon and oolichans, James saw to it that the skipper had a couple of dozen cans of salmon aboard. By May the following year he had a reply from Barrack, dated Sydney, 21st February 1868:

> Dear Sir:
> The Fraser River salmon in half barrels well packed and in such condition as I delivered mine will always command a good price if not imported in too large quantity at a time, say not over 200 half barrels. Your Ouhilans, I'm afraid are a failure in this market . . . About the salmon in tins, it is a complete success. As regards being in good condition every one of the dealers pronounced them as the best they had ever tasted in tins. I gave away a dozen to make them known. The other dozen I sold at 2s. 3d. a tin. The mistake with them was being in two lb. tins and in future you must export only in one lb. tins for this market. I think you might safely count on getting 15s. 6d. to 17s. per dozen for the one lb. tins, and get them done up in more showy colour — say bright red or blue.[2]

Both foreign and home market reports were favourable. When he sent a sample to the editor of the Colonist, the editorial for Friday, January 15 eulogized: "We were favoured with a can of Mr. James Syme's fresh salmon and can with perfect sincerity pronounce it to be the finest we ever tried. . . ."[3]

Perhaps it was encouragement of this sort that caused James Syme to over-produce for the underdeveloped market. Perhaps it was waste, or underestimating the cost of importing the sheets of Welsh tin-plate, or transportation difficulties — but whatever the cause, he went bankrupt before really getting started.

He returned to a depressed San Francisco in 1869 and resumed work at his old profession. By 1875 ill health caused him to move to Victoria, where he died at the age of 49 as the result of a "combination of diseases." He was a man of many talents, well esteemed in the community, successful as an architect, intelligent and devout with: "An abiding faith in divine wisdom and goodness and a sustaining hope in the mercy of a just creator".[4] And he was the first of many victims of the Circe canning industry on the Fraser, much of which was centered around New Westminster.

By 1867 — a year after Vancouver Island had been made a part of the colony of British Columbia — the town of New Westminster sat like a sore on the side of the hill. Flimsy frame buildings arose between huge stumps that had been left by the Royal Engineers' clearing crew. On the brow of the hill overlooking the river, sturdy timber stood like an array of giants surrounding the loose cluster of dwellings, sheds and shops.

Among the townsfolk the atmosphere was one of expectancy balanced by uncertainty. The Collins Telegraph line, which had reached New Westminster in time to transmit the news of President Lincoln's assassination in 1865, had been pushed through as far as the junction of the Skeena and Kispiox rivers before its goal of connecting up with the Russian system was abandoned due to the laying of the Atlantic cable. The result was that hundreds of Chinese and Indian workers were thrown out of work and some 500 skilled engineers and surveyors left the country. Sappers, cattle drivers, disillusioned miners and unemployed teamsters flowed through the city. Some turned to farming.[5] But the population of New Westminster was discouragingly low ever since her rival, Victoria, had purloined the capitalship. And so busy were the "British Columbian" and the "Daily Colonist" hurling abuse across the Gulf of Georgia between their respective cities that they had little space left in editorials or news columns for the business of Confederation which was going on elsewhere in Canada.

The Cariboo gold yields had fallen off too, and the trail through Fort Hope to Barkerville, once strewn with wagons that were loaded with wares and supplies purchased in New Westminster, was now a lonely route travelled mainly by those returning with their disillusionment. New Westminster was depressed — no doubt about it. Yet expectancy lingered on, and the sluggish commerce on main street gave ample opportunity for sagacious predictions between spits of tobacco juice.

The most obvious resource fairly waiting to be exploited was the salmon. In spite of the sermonic nagging of the "Colonist" — or perhaps on account of it — a few salteries were operating in and around New Westminster. Captain William Spring built a draughty little shed at Beachy Bay in 1863, shipping his produce mainly to the Cariboo. The following year a young Scots fisherman called Alexander Ewen came to New Westminster and joined with a Mr. Annadale in what proved to be a short-lived relationship, salting salmon on a large scale for England and Australia. When a letter in the March 17th edition of the "Colonist" protested against the operations of Annadale's firm on the grounds that it would soon deplete the Indians' supply of food, it was pointed out in a later edition that the "supply of fish is practically inexhaustible affording room for hundreds of fishing establishments. . . ."[6] — a statement tinged with historical irony.

Alex Ewen did not stay long with Annadale. He formed a partnership with James Wise and two natives of New Brunswick, Alexander Loggie and David Hennessy, who had been canning there but who were lured to the West Coast by the far-flung rumours of the great runs on the Fraser. In 1870 they built the first cannery on the Fraser River at Anniesville, 3 miles below New Westminster.

Now the massacre of fish commenced on a ferocious scale, for soon others were clambering into the industry and the river became a labyrinth of linen drift nets, rented and operated mainly by Indians who received as little as 5c per fish for their labours, or in some circumstances about $50 per month and keep themselves.

Along the banks of the ever-moving river shoddy frame buildings went up, their tall stacks belching smoke, while under the creosoted pilings tons of offal slid into the water. From all over the world and from every walk of life the canners came, rugged men of resolute spirit who were willing to take a risk in wresting a fortune from the chilly waters. Artists and architects they were — blacksmiths, druggists, miners and millers, prize-fighters and preachers, liquor merchants and grocers, farmers, surveyors, speculators and sea captains. There were Americans and Englishmen, Swedes and Finns, Easterners and Southerners, a few Jews and Irishmen and one Chinese outfit. But for some reason or other there was an overwhelming number of Scotsmen.

Many rushed in and perished in one or two seasons due to inexperience or misfortune. One packer lost his whole season's work because the cans were not cooked long enough and became "swells." All he could do was to salvage the solder by building a huge bonfire.

The partnership of Finlayson and Lane, one of the earliest outfits, lasted only one season. Finlayson bought out Lane and entered two other partnerships, both short-lived. A syndicate of Columbia River cannery men eager to get in on the Fraser purchased the remains of the business and operated it for five years before they were squeezed out through the dishonesty of their agents — not an uncommon fate in those days.

A canner's costs ran high before any returns could be expected. Before the Panama Canal opened in August, 1914, it took the old square riggers up to five months to deliver a shipment of salmon to England, a 16,500 mile trip. It might be another two months before the lot was actually sold, then there would be another lengthy waiting period before receiving payment. Most operators would not have been able to get into production if it were not for the agents who advanced the nets, twine, tin-plate, coal, solder, nails for shipping boxes, salt and stove oil, pig-tin, pig-lead, soldering flux and even the cash advances for the Chinese contractors whose herds of coolies worked frantically for as little as $1.25 a day (out of which they kept themselves).

Brokerage houses usually acted as agents. They made a profit in selling supplies to the canner, charged him interest on the advance and held a mortgage against the supplies and the pack before the fish were even within range of the fishing fleet. Besides the usual wharfage and handling, they charged 5% commission on all shipments of salmon. They handled all the insurance on the cannery itself, on the season's pack and the shipment while in transit. The agents chartered sailing vessels on their own account, bringing in supplies of all kinds for the young colony which finally became a province in 1871. In the mid-nineties the charge was £1:13:9 per ton for a full cargo of 62,743 cases, valued at $345,000.

These agents had one other lucrative tap into the canner's profits. When soldering machines superseded manual soldering sometimes the metal fingers that fed the cans into the machine would hit too hard and cause a tiny dent. Dealers began to complain about this, and also about the number of "dry" or "light" weight cans per shipment. Sometimes a case would be smashed in rough handling, and rust spots would appear on the cans, another cause for complaint. Ostensibly to placate the dealers, agents deducted as high as 3% from the total value of the shipment, and the canners had no way of knowing whether or not the agent was benefiting in the process.

All in all, the brokerage houses made the greatest fortunes out of the early salmon fishing industry. They reaped benefits without taking risks. When a cannery showed signs of weakness they simply foreclosed. Few operators escaped their domination and many fell victim to the more ruthless firms. But there were other problems to face.

Fire was a constant hazard in buildings constructed almost totally of lumber. The old Sapperton plant of Captain Edward Stamp, who was one of the earliest canners — also one of the earliest failures — changed hands several times and was finally purchased by a man named King who enjoyed its use for one season before it burned to the pilings, affording him the opportunity of abandoning salmon canning forever, a course he was probably glad to pursue. Idle plants sometimes stood for years, growing green with moss in the damp winter climate, and bleaching pale grey in the hot summer sun. A sad silence haunted the empty sheds. Then mysteriously, one would burst into flames, scorching the surrounding forest and dropping in sizzling chunks into the sea. In December, 1960 for example, Alaska Packers Plant on Point Roberts was gutted. It had been built before the turn of the century but had stood idle for over forty years.

Out of the numerous fires that consumed canneries all along the coast, one can safely conjecture that a number were started quite unintentionally.

In those early years before controls were established the Fraser was subject to violent floods. In one instance the curious circumstances might have been hilarious had they not been tinged with financial tragedy. It was in the early summer of 1894. Sudden sun had melted the winter snows and from its 90,903 square miles basin the Fraser gathered the run-off till it became a swollen torrent, tearing at its banks like some mad reptile, grumbling angrily as it carried gravel and stones through its canyons. High up the canyon wall at Hell's Gate, a tree trunk which had been there for as long as the Indians in the district could remember was lifted from its ledge and carried downstream. Into the valley rushed the wall of water spilling over its banks and inundating the low-lying land.

Holly Point cannery stood on a headland that projected some one hundred feet into the river. It got the full impact of the flood. The waters swirled about the sandy soil licking it away. Chunks of bank began to fall into the current and were quickly washed downstream. Soon the pilings that supported the front end of the building were dangling in the water, held only by the spikes driven through the floor-caps. Almost imperceptibly the massive building began to sag toward the water. Inch by inch the creaking, groaning structure leaned forward till it was at a frightful angle.

On the second floor, piled in rows from wall to wall and thirty tiers high, stood an orderly mountain of empty cans awaiting the commencement of the season. As the cannery sagged forward one or two toppled off with a clatter and rolled lazily across the floor. Slowly at first, in ones and twos, then in rows, the cans fell and slid across the floor till the building resounded with the steadily increasing din of careering cans. Then, with a sudden lurch hundreds of them seemed to jump from the pile. Helter-skelter they went across the slanting floor, hitting the front wall till with the strain of twisting and the pressure of the cans some of the boards sprang loose, and a column of cans began plopping into the water below. Tier after tier fell with a crash and slithered to the front wall. Like an animated army of tin paratroopers they filed out and went bobbing down the fast flowing river, some of them right out to sea before turbulent water filled them and they disappeared below the surface. By the time something could be done two hundred and forty thousand cans had disappeared and the front two-thirds of the cannery was a twisted mess.

Wellington cannery suffered in the same flood. Originally built on 21 acres of land, when the freshet subsided there were only fifteen acres left. Further downstream other canneries suffered from the changes in the channel. Woodward's slough, which was only six feet at low water, was naturally dredged to a depth of 50 to 60 feet while canneries at Ladner's Landing found ships could no longer come in to their wharfs due to the build-up of sediment.

With these difficulties it is not surprising that the years from James Syme's beginning of the industry on the Fraser, through its spread up-coast to the Nass, the Skeena, Rivers Inlet and Vancouver Island, are strewn with the wrecks of small outfits that rushed into the risky business and floundered. Only the most hardy, the most shrewd and energetic could hope to survive.

Markets were as unpredictable as the runs of salmon and prices varied violently from year to year. Most small outfits depended on one run of fish. If the run failed the outfit faced bankruptcy, for the season was short and there was no other line of production to which they could turn. Even within the season there were hectic fluctuations. For a week or two the scows and docks would be heaped each day with piles of slithering salmon which sometimes went rotten before they reached the cans. Once the main run passed, particularly if it were a poor year, few fish would be landed, sometimes barely enough to keep the plant working.

It took a rugged, adventuresome spirit to gamble against these odds, and the men who built the industry were daring individualists who reflected in their characters something of the wild, lawless sea and coast-line, but who in return clothed the coast with a robust, colourful coat of history. They were a new breed of salmon people.

CHAPTER **6**

The Cannery Clan

Among the early canners none was more highly respected by fishermen, shoreworkers and operators alike, than Alex Ewen. When he arrived in New Westminster to fish for Annadale back in 1864 he had little more than the clothes on his back. But he possessed a personal dynamism which counter-balanced his lack of formal education, and which eventually won for him the title, "Father of the Salmon Fishery", though not without a few set-backs.

Within a couple of years the original partnership of Hennessy, Loggie, Ewen and Wise broke apart. Loggie retired completely and returned to the East — disheartened. Ewen and Wise carried on with Hennessy as foreman and built at the junction of Front and Begbie Streets in New Westminster. Then Wise sold out, and Alex bought land on Lion Island where expenses were less and freedom greater. Here he built his famous "Lion and Cross Brand" Cannery and was well on the way to becoming one of the most prosperous businessmen in the community.

He acquired a large acreage of farm land as well as interests in the New Westminster Southern Railway and the New Westminster Gas Co., but Alex Ewen had been raised a fisherman and he never lost the common touch any more than he lost his thick Scots burr and the ruddy glow that shone above his bushy beard. He was honest and fair, though not more fair than shrewd business allowed, and like many of his contemporaries he possessed a phenomenal level of tolerance for good Scotch whisky, an ingredient which played no mean part in the building of the fishing industry. In his dealings with employees he was friendly and familiar, yet not above resorting to unconventional tactics of persuasion. Once he almost set fire to "China House."

Every cannery had its "China House." Droves of Chinese labourers had migrated from the United States during the Fraser Gold rush of 1858 and by 1870, in spite of the imposition of a head tax and a law which allowed one immigrant for every fifty tons of freight, many were coming directly from China. It is estimated that between the years 1881 and 1884 the Canadian Pacific Railway brought over 15,000 Chinese to labour on the building of the railroad. They worked for a mere subsistence allowance at this and as domestic servants, shoemakers, pedlars, cooks, farm-hands, labourers and gardeners. Thousands of them worked each summer at the canneries where they kept to themselves, perhaps one hundred and fifty or two hundred together in the huge shed-like building provided. This was "China House."

Because few of them ever learned to speak English and because they were all men, and therefore did not easily settle down into domestic life nor mix with other people, they were surrounded with an aura of mystery which few could penetrate. Few ever tried. For the most part they were treated as chattels, units of energy to be poured into the production pot. Even their own countrymen, the Chinese contractors who were fortunate enough to have some education and who could speak English, exploited them.

The contractor agreed with the cannery on a price for the season's work based on an estimated number of cases, then hired the coolies to do the labour for as little as possible, making a handsome profit for himself. It was actually a refined form of slavery. Sometimes the contractor would disappear, perhaps return to China, just before the end of the season and the poor wretches would be left with no wages for the whole summer's effort. Eventually these Chinese, along with the Japanese, both of whom were welcomed into the country in order to be exploited, became the target for a vicious anti-Asiatic movement which left a conspicuous blemish upon the history of the province, and which from time to time was to erupt into violence.

Alex Ewen's attitude was no better and no worse than that prevailing towards these unfortunate creatures, and so when they refused to go to work one day at the height of the season on account of some grievance, he flew into a rage. Across to the cannery store he sped and returned with a four gallon can of stove oil. He strode right up in front of China House, shaking his fist at the windows from which furtive glances were being cast. Inside a quiet rumble of excitement could be heard gathering volume.

"Goddam you!" shouted Ewen. "I'll make you come out of there. I'll burn you out — Goddam Chinamen!" and with that he punched a hole in the can and began to splash the coal-oil against the side of the building, working his way along the side, cursing in rich round syllables as he went. Before he reached the back of the building there was an unearthly yell from hundreds of throats and China House began to empty itself. Wildly gesticulating Chinese climbed over each other in the effort to get out. They were brandishing their huge butcher knives and yelling excitedly in their own language, so that for a moment Alex was not sure of their intent. But they fled in a body right into the cannery and before long the machinery was rolling again.

On another occasion he threatened to load them all onto a scow and cut it adrift out on the Gulf. The Chinese were poor sailors. Out of the thousands that were employed in the fishing industry few ever went fishing, so the thought of being set adrift out on the Straits of Georgia soon persuaded them that the meagre benefits of China House were more to be desired than a watery grave.

Alex Ewen could be violent and stubborn in labour relations but most of the time as he walked about the plant, he was greeted with admiration and affectionate respect for he knew most of his men and women by first name. None was more admiring than a little Indian girl named Ada Ellerd. Whenever she was fortunate enough to have ten cents to spend she would hunt for him and hold out a sticky candy in her filthy little fist. Ewen would rather have had a plug of tobacco, but he always took the candy just to please Ada. She had fallen off the wharf one summer into the river and though he could swim no more than a keg of spikes, he had jumped in after her gum boots and all, and somehow managed to get her to shore.

Ewen liked to watch the deft, rhythmic movements of the workers, but one of the fellows pitching was obviously a new man and Alex grew more impatient as he watched the awkward action. Ewen knew well the knack of handling the single-pronged fork, for he had pitched thousands of sockeye himself. He knew that an experienced hand could keep the fish flying in a steady arc into the bin, being careful not to puncture the flesh, but to jab only in the head or tail. The newcomer was doing his best but he was slow, and often the fish would fall off the pew before the toss and would land half way, thus making extra work and extra handling. Finally Ewen could stand it no longer. Exasperated, he jumped forward and grabbed the pew from the lad's hands.

fast slitter could do up to 2,000 fish in a ten hour day.

Ewen liked to watch the deft, rhythmic movements of the workers, but one of the fellows pitching was obviously a new man and Alex grew more impatient as he watched the awkward action. Ewen knew well the knack of handling the single-pronged fork, for he had pitched thousands of sockeye himself. He knew than an experienced hand could keep the fish flying in a steady arc into the bin, being careful not to puncture the flesh, but to jab only in the head or tail. The newcomer was doing his best but he was slow, and often the fish would fall off the pew before the toss and would land half way, thus making extra work and extra handling. Finally Ewen could stand it no longer. Exasperated, he jumped forward and grabbed the pew from the lad's hands.

"Here, give me that thing," he thundered. "That's no way to

pitch fish," and he leapt into the pile of slimy carcases determined to pitch with a fury. In his haste he lost his footing. Frantically, he fought to maintain balance. Fish flew in every direction as he kept on pitching while at the same time his feet were dancing in the knee-deep mass of moving bodies till finally, after some of the most fantastic contortions, he came to a stop sitting in the slime with fish sliding around him up to the waist. Quietly he handed the lad the pew and climbed out of the mess, coated with scales.

In spite of these displays, Alexander Ewen was one of the most magnanimous men to be found on the Coast. More than once he assisted others whom he had employed to establish themselves as his competitors. David Hennessy, for example, was for many years his cannery foreman and George Alexander his net boss. When an opportunity opened for them to get into business themselves, he financed them without hesitation.

Daniel Munn was his bookkeeper for years, but when the Haig cannery went up for sale Ewen put up most of the money and between them they purchased it. Later, they built the Sea Island Cannery on the North Arm of the Fraser, and again most of the capital came from Alexander Ewen.

Though it was not common knowledge, Daniel Munn had designs on one of Alex's three fair daughters, or at least made a good showing in this direction. For years the girls had been coming around the cannery during the summer. Back home at New Westminster father would suddenly announce that the family could come to the cannery for the day. There would be a hectic rush and mother would get one of her migraine headaches, but when they were all piled onto "the Buz", better known as "Ewen's Buggy", she would sit up in front in the cramped cabin and sing ballads and folk-songs as they chugged down the river to Lion Island. Once there, the girls made a bee-line for the cook-house with its lye-bleached plank floor where the Chinese cook would beckon them into the kitchen.

"You likee cookie? You likee cookie?" he would ask with a broad grin, and invite them to lift the lid of his cookie barrel and help themselves to a piece of glazed pie or sponge cake with currants on top. Next it was out to the night watchman's garden armed with salt on a piece of paper, to pick fresh vegetables and dip them into the salt, none of which affected their appetites for dinner, for it seemed to the girls that food eaten on stools at the end of the long table twenty minutes before the crew came crashing in, was the most wonderful meal in the whole world.

This was when they were younger, of course. When Adelaide blossomed into an attractive young woman, Daniel Munn was very attentive, and all the well-informed of New Westminster were confident that wedding bells were about to peal.

Daniel was an industrious fellow with a good business head. He and the prospective father-in-law were involved jointly in several enterprises besides fishing — including the building of the Kaslo and Slocan Railway in the Kootenay mining area. Everyone was quite surprised, therefore, when Daniel Munn sold out and moved to Montreal where he married the daughter of a wealthy merchant, a union from which there was one daughter, born blind, who became the internationally famous pianist, Mary Munn.

Many names flit across the scene of those first years, names like Stamp, King, Lane, Pike, Nelson and others. But the clan who came and stayed was composed of men like Alexander Ewen, men of stamina and determination who would not flinch in the face of overwhelming difficulties.

There was Tom Ladner and William, his older brother. They were English farmers who had reached British Columbia via California after crossing the continent in a covered wagon, the first overland party to succeed following the ill-fated Donner party's attempt. The brothers spent some time in the Cariboo country, came to the Fraser and bought 640 acres of delta marshland, dyked and drained it and had a stretch of the richest farmland in Canada.

Tom Ladner was about five feet, five inches in height and almost as much in circumference. Weighing around two hundred and forty-eight pounds, he was said to resemble the shape of a

47

well-known brand of Scotch whisky to which he was partial. Indeed, from Victoria to well up the Fraser Valley one could enter a saloon and order a "drap o' Tam Ladner" and the proper brand would be produced on the instant. Tom Ladner and his friend James A. Laidlaw, a quiet Scot who retired early due to ill health, opened the famous Delta Canning Company at Ladner's Landing in 1879 and both went on to own several canneries.

Another ex-Cariboo miner, whose name is stamped indelibly on the coast through canning was E. A. Wadhams. Once while mushing out from the Cariboo along a winding trail in the Fraser Canyon, he was buried alive under an avalanche. For hours his friends worked in vain to find him and were on the point of giving up several times. Each time they stopped his wife begged them to keep digging. All the while Wadhams was pinned in by tons of snow, with a small air pocket about his head, so that he could not move and was afraid to shout lest he be smothered. He could hear them give him up for lost, then his wife's pleading with them to continue digging, until at last he was hauled out stiff with cold and badly shaken, but otherwise unharmed. As well as his wife's persistence Wadhams' own self-control had a lot to do with his rescue that day.

Financial casualties were frequent among the early canners. Many were eliminated from the industry before they became known. For example in 1883 thirteen canneries belched and fussed along the banks of the Fraser River, but the next two years there were only six operating plants. It was surprising with what apparent ease others were able to acquire a fortune. Charles C. Windsor started out as cannery tinsmith for Alex Ewen. When Inverness Cannery was built on the Skeena River it needed a foreman and Charlie got the job upon Ewen's recommendation. In 1889 he met a man who told a good story, so good in fact that he convinced Charlie he had $10,000.00 ready to invest. Windsor persuaded him to go into partnership — Mr. Hobson to provide most of the money and he to provide the know-how. When the cannery, located at Garry Point on the Fraser, was well under way and Windsor owed money to everybody in town, Hobson confessed that he did not have the capital he had claimed. Windsor lost no time. He borrowed $25 to pay his fare to Victoria where he forced Hobson to go into Turner-Beeton and Co. with him to see if they would back the project. He had to borrow another $20 to pay his hotel bill, but when they left Victoria they had $4,000 advance with which to keep creditors at bay. That season they packed 13,716 cases of sockeye, paid off all their debts including Turner-Beeton, then sold out to Anglo British Columbia Packers for $35,000. In 1893 when Garry Point site was regarded as useless on account of erosion damage, Windsor bought the property back for $5,000 and erected the Gulf of Georgia Cannery with which he did extremely well.

Others acquired fortunes by wading through much more arduous circumstances. A man who actually came back from ruin that was instigated through the dishonesty of his agents, was Marshall English, one of the most colourful characters among the canners. Strikingly handsome, with a sharp wit and a keen mind, he was admired by all who knew him. He claimed to be one of the "F.F.V." (First Families of Virginia) and was in fact a cousin of Dr. Thomas Dunn English, author of the popular ballad, "Ben Bolt".

Marshall English's career was one of extremes. He came to California via Panama, mined himself into wealth in the Nevada region, then moved to San Francisco where he lost practically everything in the 1875 stock market slump. What he had left he invested in salmon canning and with the backing of a man he thought to be his friend, he was hopeful of recovering some of his previous losses. At a time when he could not stand the strain he was confronted with enormous spoilage claims from his agent friend. When he went to San Francisco to discuss the matter he was told that he would have to fold up.

English had his name published on the passenger list to Victoria but immediately took off across the continent and hence to Liverpool. With the aid of a lawyer he contacted the British buyers and discovered that they had not made the spoilage claims at all. He was being fleeced by his friend the agent. Armed with this information he returned to Canada only to discover that foreclosure proceedings were under way.

The Judge was the notorious Begbie. Years before, William D. English, Marshall's brother, had used Begbie for the brunt of a joke when both of them were up in the Cariboo country. Begbie had never forgotten it. Much to the surprise of the whole court, including the prosecution, he found in favour of the plaintiff and English was stripped of his property.

Marshall English was not the type to give up easily. He appealed, and consequently a Royal Commission was sent to investigate the company. At the hearing, English was represented by his cousin, W. W. Foote, but he could barely contain himself. As witnesses for the company in question gave evidence English would lean over to his cousin and whisper, "That's a damned lie," and begin to explain the real facts. Foote was listening but not taking any notes. Each time English leaned over to whisper, he hushed him up. At last the lawyer drew out a silver dollar, handed it to his cousin and said, "Marsh, go and get me four twenty-five cent cigars, will you?" English was rising to go when Foote threw over his shoulder, "And don't come back till you smoke them all!" From that point on, English was quiet. When it came time for Foote to examine the witnesses he simply asked for adjournment.

Marshall English was beginning to wonder if he had chosen the right man to represent him. Next morning Foote stood up and without a note began to quote verbatim from the evidence of the previous day, pointing out the inconsistencies until he was right under the nose of the trembling witness, waving a threatening finger and demanding the truth. The witness broke down and confessed that he had been bribed to give false testimony, and Marshall English regained his property.

English had started out in partnership with John Adair and S. S. Martin, building the first really mechanized cannery on the coast of Brownsville opposite New Westminster. However, after he became sole owner he moved to Steveston near the river's mouth, where large ocean going vessels could come right to the wharf to be loaded, and where it got the name that is still famous, "Phoenix Cannery".

Once at Phoenix Cannery he came close to being chopped to pieces by an irate mob of armed Chinese workers. The "Chinamen," as they were called, were often the brunt of jokes and teasing which sometimes went too far. One of the white workers who was reputed to have a mean streak had been picking on a Chinese worker for most of the season until one day the Oriental could take no more and turned to the bully in protest, only to be knocked to the floor with a heavy fist. As he fell he struck his head on a table. At the sight of the blood gushing from his head, the rest of the Chinese started toward the offender.

The foreman, a short distance away, grabbed an iron tray and brought it down on the head of the first man, believing this to be the fastest method of preventing a row. That did it. With raised butcher knives they came in a pack, closing in on the two white men who suddenly made a dash for the door. The whole howling pack was after them with screams of rage and vengeance. Just as the two men dived through the door, Marshall English was about to enter.

"Run for your life!" they yelled. "The Chinamen have gone berserk!" In a moment he saw what was happening. English stepped inside the cannery, quickly slid the bolt and stood with his back to the door facing the growling mob who threatened to cut him to pieces if he did not let them get at the escapees. There were a few tense moments when he could almost feel the breeze of their waving knives. They were wild with fury and determined to get revenge. But eventually he managed to calm them down by speaking through their "bossman". When they reluctantly shuffled back to their benches, English went out and fired the men on the spot.

Another well known character among the canners was Jacob Todd. Jacob Hunter Todd came to British Columbia from Eastern Canada through the Cariboo country as an itinerant trader. When the Cariboo excitement was over he crossed to Victoria, entered the wholesale grocery business and made a fortune in a very short time. In the process he acquired the reputation of being shrewd even beyond the normal run of Scots merchants, a reputation which he brought with him into the canning business when in 1882 he built Richmond Cannery on the North Arm. This pawkiness lent point to more than one tale in which Todd figured. In the Doyle papers, a casual record left by an Irish adventurer, the story is told of how Jacob Todd commandeered two Indians who fished for him to row him from Richmond Cannery up to New Westminster. There he was to catch the weekly steamer across to Victoria. The river, Doyle tells us, was in freshet at the time and the going was hard, but the Indian lads were strong, and they looked forward to a good meal and a hotel room when they got to New Westminster. It was dark when they arrived, and as they clomped along the boardwalk behind the wealthy Todd, their hopes were set high for the pay-off.

They were passing a grocery store with its wares spread out on counters for late shoppers, when Todd jerked to a halt. Reaching across to a packet of hard-tack, he drew out four pieces and gave two each to the lads who had worked so hard to transport him up the river.

"Here you are, boys," he said, "There's your supper," and with that he turned on his heel and left them standing, bewildered. Doyle further records that when the news reached the cannery, there was ugly grumbling and strike talk among the workers, and indeed there might have been serious trouble if the local manager, unknown to the owner, had not paid the men handsomely under the camouflage of "fish prices".

When the steamer arrived in New Westminster everyone congregated at the wharf whether or not they had freight. It was a weekly festival of conversation, friendly hilarity and social visiting. On one occasion Tom Ladner was at the rail of the steamer as she edged in, and on the dock, among others, was this same Henry Doyle. The conversation as he records it, followed these lines.

"Hello there, Todd," shouted the corpulent Ladner from the rail, "and how are things with you?"

"Very well, thank you — and how are things in Victoria?"

"Just fine," said Ladner, "though I hear you have competition over there now."

By now, Doyle recalls, not without a hint of malicious glee, everyone on the wharf as well as on deck, was listening to the conversation with at least one ear, eager to catch a choice piece of news.

"Yes sir," said Ladner, "I hear there is someone over there just as mean and tight as you are."

Peals of laughter broke forth from the crowded wharf. Todd forced an uncomfortable smile, doing his best to be a good sport.

"Well now, I wonder who on earth that could be," he replied.

"Your son, Charlie," replied Ladner and again the wharf roared with mirth, just as the gang plank dropped.

Understandably Jacob Todd was not popular among the other canners but he was a successful business man and was one of the few to weather the gathering storm by which the industry was to be pummelled, the only one of the early canners whose name is still in the industry today, though the firm no longer is owned by the family.

And so the cannery clan on the Fraser grew. It was composed of colourful characters who often could be found staining the plank walk in front of Tolmie's Hotel with their cigar ash and tobacco juice, but who might also be found pitching fish or quelling a riot, mending a machine or fighting a fire. They were men of action as well as acumen.

By 1890, thirty-one canneries were in operation and their total annual output was 409,464 cases. Every sockeye producing area was open to exploitation and the character of the coast had changed, invaded as it was by the clanking of cans, the thumping of presses, the hiss of steam. The sea air hung heavy in the valleys, laden with the stench of fish flesh and the tide came back to swallow the excreta of the hives of agitation that were the cannery communities.

The men who built the industry, too numerous to list, were pioneers in the true sense of the word, and if some of them made a fortune they received the just reward of risk. But now even greater changes were poised in the hand of fate ready to be flung upon the seventeen thousand miles of gnarled shore, and upon those who dared to wrest a living from its waters, changes which were to break the back of many companies and which were to seriously endanger the supplies of salmon forever.

CHAPTER 7

The Big Run

Up to the twenty-third of July in the year 1897 everything was normal on the Fraser River. The sun beat down on the mud-stained water making it look like molten silver. Around the canneries the usual raucous rhythm of work and amusement was under way; Indian children dashing helter-skelter with green running noses, lethargic old men propped against clapboard walls, clusters of Chinese jabbering excitedly on mundane topics as they trudged from the cannery to China House. Everything was normal — the usual strong stink of dumped offal, the nets drooped across the rocks, the rows of Indian shacks and the smarter Japanese houses with the bread-earner's fishing license-number painted on a board above the door so that if a boat was lost at sea the proper family could be notified. There were the usual drunks weaving miraculously along the narrow plank walks, and down at the fish wharf the catches were about normal for that stage of the season. Then on the 23rd of July something phenomenal happened.

Back in 1887 an outbreak of typhoid fever had been attributed to unsanitary conditions around the canneries and to the dumping of offal — about 9 million lbs. of it each season on the Fraser alone. The result was that a federal commission was set up, headed by an Ontario-raised man called Newcombe, undoubtedly an intelligent, conscientious, industrious and devoted servant of the people but one who knew practically nothing about fishing. For instance he could not be convinced that Pacific salmon died after spawning. One outcome of this commission was that a limit of 500 boats was set to fish the Fraser, with Indians to have preference.

This was a shallow solution to a deep problem, but it suited the existing operators for it gave them a virtual monopoly, making it difficult for newcomers to break into the industry since each fisherman was licensed through the canneries. A few individual licenses were held, but for the most part the cannery was allotted a maximum of twenty licenses which they would dole out, and with which they could exploit the fisherman. Some companies were even known to build ghost canneries, which never operated, in order to obtain a greater share of the 500 licenses issued.

While this was going on the British Columbia government was circulating attractive brochures throughout Britain, encouraging immigration to the land of plenty, one of the greatest drawing cards being the abundant fisheries. When a number of Scots fishermen made the long journey they discovered that they could not get licenses to fish and were forced to return home.

It was not until 1892 that the restriction was lifted, with an ensuing rush on the part of both fishermen and canners to get in on the predicted heavy run of 1893. That year *was* a good one and so were the next few seasons, so that even those without experience blundered along making attractive profits. As the 1897 season opened the price of sockeye was eight cents each with the stipulation that if there was a glut the cannery would be obliged to take only 200 from each fisherman.

This is how things stood until the twenty-third of July. On that day, boats fishing far out off the mouth of the river dropped their nets into the water and within minutes had to pick them up for fear the weight of fish would sink them. Loaded to the gunwales, they hoisted their patchy sails and raced for the canneries, hoping to unload before the inside fishermen made similar catches and the two-hundred-fish limit would be imposed. But they were not fast enough. The fish beat them there. Already the inside fishermen had landed their catches and the cannery floors were loaded.

So anxious were the canners to obtain full packs that they took every fish they could get that first day. After all there was no telling how long the run would last. Scows, fish-wharfs, packers, cannery floors and all available receptacles were crammed full of the bright, silvery sockeyes, so that by the following day the two-hundred limit had to be strictly imposed.

On the other hand, fishermen were so desperate to get rid of their catches they voluntarily dropped the price to two cents per fish, and eventually thousands of choice sockeyes were being offered at one-quarter of a cent each, with no takers. Fishermen no longer bothered to go out. Teams of three and four worked together using one net which they dropped off the end of the wharf and picked up almost immediately, filled with fighting fish, enough for each man's limit.

Desperately the canneries tried to keep up with the incredible harvest. It was dreary work inside the damp, noisy cannery with its whining belts and whirling fly wheels, its narrow pipes dropping down from overhead mains bringing ceaseless streams of cold water to the work stalls. Long rows of Chinese "slitters" and Indian "washers" shifted from foot to aching foot at their slimy benches working methodically to the point of exhaustion, their fingers raw and ankles swollen from doing extra shifts. Around the circular knifed cutting machine heaps of finely ground flesh piled up, while chunks of salmon tumbled from the draining tables onto the floor, to be kicked beneath the benches or squashed under gum-boots. Weary fillers wearing dusters and smocks, rubber aprons and canvas gloves leaned against the tables, and although their hands moved like those of figures in a speeded-up movie, filling the passing cans, it seemed to make no impression on the piles of salmon wheeled to them in boxes on wooden buggies. Steam and odorous fumes mingled with the stench of raw fish. The din of clattering cans and the clanking of the new soldering machines pounded on the workers' nerves.

Accidents occurred with increased frequency as fatigue slipped over into carelessness. And still the salmon came.

The waste was terrific. Waste was in fact a characteristic of early salmon fishing. For the first forty years of the industry species other than sockeye or red spring were not intentionally caught, and when they were, as was inevitable, they were forked overboard. How many millions of perfectly good Cohoe Pinks and Chums were wantonly thrown away no one will ever know.

Accidents sometimes accounted for spoilages. Alex C. Anderson, fishery inspector for British Columbia, a very colourful and well-known personality who held various posts including chief trader for the Hudson's Bay Company, postmaster at Victoria, first collector of customs in British Columbia and commissioner for the settlement of the Indian Land question (still not settled) referred in his report of 1877 to the accidental destruction of salmon catches. In one instance Finlayson and Lane overcaught and were unable to process all the fish before they went bad. The hot weather was conspicuously noted as a contributing culprit. At Marshall English's cannery a scow-load of sockeyes was ruined when an accidental discharge by a steamer tied alongside scalded the whole load. But the restraint with which Anderson mentioned wastage in his reports was more indicative of his temperament than of the conditions in fishing.[1]

Incredible as it seems, around the seventies the Colonist was levelling tirades against the operators for using only the bellies and throwing away backs. The inspector of fisheries in 1882 notified the canners that this practice must stop. "No thoughtful person can defend this practice," he said, "while there are so many thousands in the old country who would gladly buy it as an article of food." With what must have seemed to him to be deep insight he went on to suggest that the backs be used as food for the Indians.[2]

Even prime, whole sockeyes were thrown overboard from time to time when a sudden rush found the canneries ill-prepared and unable to handle the catches.

But nothing equalled the devastation and destruction of that summer of 1897. Fishermen who had overcaught the limit were forced to dump their surplus overboard, and nearly everyone caught more than the two-hundred per day. At the wharfs, yesterday's fish which had not been canned were forked into the water to make room for today's catch.

Down to the bottom of the river the dead fish plunged, hundreds of thousands of them, seven pounds of rich protein each with millions of eggs captured in the sepulchres of their body cavities. Then bloated, ugly and putrid they rose to the surface. The incoming tide and prevailing wind kept them in the river, even carrying some further up-stream before they were deposited on the banks, where along with tons of offal they continued to rot. From Garry Point at the mouth of the river, for several miles back, the shore was lined with a twenty-four inch layer of stinking, rotten fish, in some places as much as two hundred feet wide. Around every cannery conditions were similar and for miles the country was sick with the fetid breath of the decomposing mess which, owing to low tides, remained well into the Fall. The few attempts to bury rotten salmon in trenches were negligible in effect.

For many years one of the most contentious problems of the fishery was pollution of the adjacent waters. The canneries simply allowed waste to slide into the "chuck", believing that old mother nature would carry it away. The commission set up in 1887 had been in response to concern over this. In 1892 another commission was appointed to investigate the salmon fishing with special reference to the disposal of refuse. Regulations were imposed, but were not observed. The following year the whole adult population of Ladner's Landing, forty-eight in number, signed a petition of protest against the dumping of waste products from the canneries.[3] One farmer complained:

> "My farm is just two miles from the Delta Cannery on the slough running up from Point Roberts. When the tide runs up it goes with a pretty big current and takes everything right up to the head of the slough and then it stays there. . . . Since these

> canneries have been there we have had much typhoid fever.
> Right along this slough we have had seventeen cases of fever
> this last summer, four cases in my own house alone. . . . And
> Mr. Colhoun — his farm is opposite mine — he had five cases
> in his house.[4]

Several attempts were made to utilize waste products. Two
Frenchmen established an operation near Ladner's Landing in
1888, but it is reported the smell of the factory was so strong the
settlers in the area were responsible for its termination by fire.
Joseph Spratt set up his famous "Ark" in English Bay and
succeeded in making an oil which had to be dumped when it
went rancid, with the result that the waters were poisoned for
days. Tom Ladner and R. P. Rithet also built an offal factory
opposite Delta cannery. Their guano won an award at the Chica-
go Columbian Exposition in 1892, but they were too early with
their product and were forced to offer the whole works as a gift
to anyone who would take it away. There was no market. So
problems of contamination and waste were by no means new to
the inhabitants of the lower Fraser and vicinity. But never had
they experienced anything like the summer of the big run, in
1897.

From the twenty-third of July to the fifteenth of August the
run continued unabated. Old Indians wagged their heads and
rubbed their chins in wonder. Though it was common knowledge
that every fourth year for some strange reason the salmon came
in greater abundance, never had there been such a run of fish.
At first there was jocund excitement over the bonanza, but this
mood soon gave way to weariness and to a sense of uneasiness
over the accumulation of carrion along the shores, and even the
gleeful grin of the canners was soon marred with a shadow of
anxiety.

It was inevitable that the gigantic run should have an adverse
effect upon the market. Some sold their entire packs ahead of
the season for $4 per case of one-pound tails, a cut of approxi-
mately 25% from the previous season's price. They were fortunate, or wise, for those who held on till the end of the season

were very glad to get rid of salmon at $3 per case, though even at this price most outfits managed to make money. They had purchased the raw product at rock bottom prices. The boom was on. Nevertheless, the existence of many an outfit was precarious.

One result of the 1897 season, due in part to the fatigue of workers and the inexperience of some canners, was the large quantities of tainted and off-quality fish that reached the markets, thus slowing sales so that when next season opened there were stocks of salmon still unsold. This combined with unexpected large runs in the following seasons and the influx of numerous incompetent, speculative operators, caused further retardation of sales and depression of prices just at a time when costs were rising sharply due to increases in the price of tin and the organization of the fishermen. The "big run" hailed by all as an opportunity for high profits was in reality the beginning of the end for many canners.

CHAPTER **8**

Three Strikes You're Out

There had been a lot of fun back in July 1893 when members of the newly formed Fraser River Fishermen's Protective and Benevolent Association met to air and organize their gripes. Chief Cranberry Jack and Chief Capilano George exulted in the opportunity of demonstrating their ancient dramatic and oratory skills to the white men by strutting across the stage miming the detested cannery owners and voicing resentments through an interpreter. Everyone enjoyed the show, so they decided to strike — the first one in the history of the most strike-scarred industry in Canada. But it fizzled out and the Association failed to survive this first attempt at self assertion, partly due to the lack of co-operation between the various factions; Japanese, Chinese, Whites and Indians. In fact one reason for the formation of the Association was opposition to the growing number of Japanese fishermen. It was hardly likely that they would co-operate.

Even the canners were not unanimous in their stand against the strikers. Alexander Ewen who had been a fisherman himself and who knew the backbreaking, miserable toil involved, refused to comply with the six cent price agreed upon by the recently formed Canners Association. He insisted on paying at least eight cents and wanted to maintain the ten cent per fish level of the previous season. Consequently the 1893 strike was conspicuous for its lack of strength on both sides.

Nevertheless some form of union was long overdue, for prices were ridiculously low, even though on off years, especially when labour was scarce during the Yukon gold rush, competition between packers boosted the price as high as thirty cents per fish for those who owned their own boats.

In the beginning nearly all the fishermen were Indians, but following the Fraser and Cariboo gold scurries more and more whites took to the sea hoping to find the bonanza that had eluded them in the interior. Meantime, Japanese immigrants came in increasing numbers, settling mainly around Steveston, and turned to fishing for a living. It is estimated that by 1900 some 4,000 Japanese were in the industry. The return fare was only about twenty-five dollars and in the beginning many went back to their homeland after the season. At that time naturalization in Canada did not deprive them of Japanese national status. It resumed upon their return. As time went on, great numbers stayed behind and made Canada their home. They were industrious, clean, law-abiding citizens, but they became scapegoats for the ills and frustrations of the white population for many years, and the culminating act against them in 1942 may never be eradicated from the Canadian conscience.

Added to this was the annual migration of hundreds of American fishermen who, even after the legislation of 1892 limiting licenses to British Subjects, with the aid of the canneries managed to come north and find employment reaping a harvest from yet unspoiled Canadian waters.

It is not surprising therefore that during the winter of 1899-1900 two separate but co-operating unions emerged at New Westminster and Vancouver, both of them organized by Joseph H. Watson of the Vancouver Trades Council. Watson was a liberal but the leadership soon passed into the hands of a stormy ex-seaman called Frank Rogers who was a fanatical member of the United Socialist Labour Party and whose violent career ended some years later, when in the pursuit of his favourite pastime, namely—striking—he was ambushed and murdered by a group of C.P.R. thugs. Under Frank Rogers' fiery leadership the fishermen went on strike in 1900 and a sort of ludicrous terror reigned for three weeks while each side tested the strength of the other.

The young city of Vancouver had not seen such excitement and crowds since the fire. A procession was led by the colourful Fort Simpson Indian band pounding out their repertoire of rousing tunes. Following them were officials of the Vancouver Trades and Labour Council and behind that a long wavy line of 1,000 fishermen and sympathizers. At the corner of Hastings and Cambie streets the milling crowd steadied long enough to listen to speeches rendered from the steps of the old courthouse in the usual vernacular of labour language, on the evils of the capitalists and the long-suffering patience of the fishermen which had finally come to an end. The strike was already a week old, but they would not fish till the canners met their demands for twenty cents per fish and recognition of their organization.

Meantime the canners were busily executing their own particular brand of self-righteous autocracy. In January of that year they had re-organized the old British Columbia Salmon Packers Association into the Fraser River Canners Association with power to levy heavy fines on any outfit which did not abide by the agreements and regulations. When the fishermen went on strike they mustered their resources and decided that the finest bargaining agent they could employ was an "exhibition of authority" by having four of the cannery tugs patrol the fishing grounds, each carrying three or four special constables.

Under the false security of this demonstration of power a few fishermen were persuaded to go out. If the action was, as later admitted by Chief Constable Lister, to "test the attitude of the strikers," the cannery men were not to be disappointed. Union picket boats flying their white flags with a red 25, quickly seized one of the boats and towed it along with its occupants to the wharf at Steveston, where the unfortunate boatpuller was hauled onto a box by Rogers to be jeered at as a "scab" before being thrown about like a football as he attempted to dash through the mob.

Indignantly the canners called, "Riot!" The incident had taken place on Friday. By Monday Rogers was arrested and imprisoned and by midnight the same day, following a panicky wire to Attorney General Eberts at Victoria, and on the authority of three local J.P.'s, the militia marshalled at Vancouver. Amid a glorious chorus of boos and hisses, one hundred and sixty gallant men of the Sixth Regiment of the Duke of Connaught's Own Rifles, better remembered as the "Sockeye Fusiliers" or the "Steveston Rangers," boarded the steamer Comox for front line duty over at the wharf of Phoenix Cannery.

Meanwhile negotiations had been going on sporadically. The fishermen turned down an eighteen cents offer but when nineteen cents was suggested the eighteen-hundred-strong Japanese Benevolent Society, which had been formed independently in June of the same year, accepted and their boats began to head for the fishing grounds. There was no alternative for the whites and Indians but to accept.

In 1901 there was another strike, this time more vehement. Armed union boats patrolled the waters boarding vessels of the non-striking Japanese fishermen and any others who dared put to sea, cutting their nets to ribbons and setting boats adrift while the fishermen were put ashore at some remote point. Police boats were helpless amid the confusion. Fist and bottle fights were frequent on the waterfront, as many as seven outbreaks of violence occurring in one evening. Six Japanese fishermen were hijacked from the fishing grounds. Their boats were set adrift and they were stranded on Bowen Island, presumed lost till finally picked up by a Union Steamship Company boat.

As a result members of the patrol boat responsible for the action along with the notorious Frank Rogers and another strike leader were arrested. Fifteen charges were laid against Rogers. In Vancouver a mass meeting of fishermen was called at which the prevailing mood was so ugly that with very little provocation the men would have marched down to the old wooden jail and taken Rogers and the others by force. However the militant spirit of this strike soon fizzled out too, and one of the reasons, though union men would not like to admit it, was the recurrence of the Big Run.

Though the run of 1901 was not quite that of the previous cycle year, almost twice as many fish were processed. For by now seventy-seven canneries operated along the coast, forty-nine of them on the Fraser, and the river was crammed with 3,832 fishermen.

Counting U.S. production, five million cases of Pacific salmon were packed that season. But where were they going to sell that amount of salmon? Again the old problem of a flooded market and much poor quality depressed sales and prices. In 1897 most operators had made a profit because they had procured the raw fish for practically nothing. But now initial costs could not be whittled down by peeling off the fishermen's pay.

The industry was in trouble. Packers had large amounts of capital tied up, and most of them went deeply into debt in order to get into production each season. At the time of the bonanza sawmills would advance lumber for the shipping boxes. The small marine yards that built the fishing skiffs agreed to wait till the end of the season for payment. Supply houses extended credit for nets, twines and the myriad necessary accoutrements. New soldering machines, cutting machines, box nailing machines could be paid for when the pack was sold. Even the fishermen had to wait, sometimes for months, to receive a final settlement. (They still do.) With slow returns the loans were not retired properly and interest mounted. Banks were nervous about further loans and the well-established firms were worried over weak operations going into receivership and being sold for a song, thus creating fresh competition. Besides, there was growing anxiety over the increasing percentage of Canadian fish being caught by American Packers on Puget Sound as the schools passed through United States waters.

Many smaller outfits could not stand the strain. Wursburg and Company was a firm which entered the business with a lack of capital and an even greater deficiency in knowledge. The Fraser River Canners' Association eventually bought their Albion

Island plant from its creditors and later resold it. Cleeve Canning and Cold Storage was owned by Sir Thomas Cleeve, an Irish baronet. It lasted only a short time. Westminster Packing Company was a wealthy Chinese firm under the leadership of a highly respected resident of New Westminster called Lam Tung. The outfit made more money contracting in Chinese labour than they ever did in canning. In 1911 Sir Robert Doughty built the Alliford Bay plant at Skidegate Inlet on Queen Charlotte Islands. It was perhaps the most ambitious private attempt ever made to exploit the B.C. fisheries, involving an initial investment of $1,250,000. It included a three-line cannery, a fertilizer plant built of reinforced concrete, and a modern fish-oil refinery. Machinery alone cost in the neighbourhood of $110,000. It was all sold to Sir Thomas Lipton for $50,000. The plant saw very little operation.

One of the most fascinating failures on the coast was the monstrosity called "Spratt's Ark." When Joseph Spratt's wife died in 1881, he decided to retire from active control of the Albion Iron Works and to spend time developing an idea he had for a floating cannery. On Christmas Eve of the following year his employees gave him the proverbial "testimonial dinner."

No doubt about it, Jo Spratt had been an honest and successful man. Born in England in 1835 he had gone to California in the Gold Rush days and with the proceeds of his adventures established a foundry in San Francisco. After awhile he moved to Victoria where in 1862 he purchased a couple of lots at the corner of Chatham and Discovery Streets and built a small foundry with an 8 h.p. steam engine that drove all the machinery in the works. Since then he had had the pleasure of watching the business grow beyond his wildest dreams. But he was happy to step aside at last, to see his son Charles take over management, and to have an opportunity to experiment with something new.

All that winter the yards at Albion Iron Works resounded with the ring of hammered metal and the whine of sawn lumber. Gradually the "Ark" took shape, till one damp morning towards the end of April a devoted knot of people, who were willing to

67

brace themselves against the five o'clock chill that rose from the water, watched her being launched.

She was an unwieldy big scow, 140 feet long with a 33 foot 6 inch beam. On the main deck stood a two-storey building, the upper floor fitted as quarters for captain and crew. These quarters were located, apparently, in such a way as to take full advantage of the various scents that rose in billowing clouds of steam from the floor below, where fish oil was to be manufactured along with the canning of salmon; neither of which was actually accomplished with any degree of success. Down in the hold lurked a 30 h.p. engine run on steam from two 50" boilers, and from the engine a ponderous shaft thrust itself through the stern. Just in case the steam power failed or fatigued at an inopportune moment a mast was fitted ahead of the deck houses and from it hung a square sail and jib, a very wise precaution though the stack at the stern soon had the sails as black as the rest of the craft. She could by no stretch of imagination be called a graceful creation. But who cared about grace so long as she made money, and with her mobility Spratt had no doubt that she would do well.

On Saturday, June 16th, 1883, at 6:30 a.m. she churned into motion with a sound like a damaged calliope, flags flying and towing a long line of fishing skiffs that looked like an entourage of page boys following an overweight duchess. But the "Ark" was a failure as a cannery.

The first modification was to remove the fish oil refinery for it was found that there was not enough space for canning, and when they did get a pack there was no place to store it. She was almost impossible to navigate. Once when crossing between Vancouver and Victoria the "Ark" was swept sideways down the Gulf of Georgia by a light Norwester. It eventually wheezed into Victoria harbour after 39 hours full-steam ahead. To overcome this power deficiency she had to be accompanied by a tug that nuzzled along like a hen-pecked consort and added expense to the operation.

Just the same "Spratt's Ark" fussed her way into the heart of

68

every B.C. coast dweller. After being rejuvenated with an additional engine she went into the freighting business and carried the bricks from Vancouver Island that rebuilt Vancouver following the disastrous fire of 1886. She changed hands many times, working on salvage operations about the old *San Pedro,* in quarry work on the North Arm of Burrard Inlet. In the raucous days of the Klondike she carried everything from coal to straw mattresses into Wrangell, and she saw service as a ferry barge across Burrard Inlet before there was a bridge. Some say her bones are still in the mud on the shore of North Vancouver. Others claim that she ended her days in Wrangell. But in either case as a cannery Spratt's Ark was the most beloved failure on the coast, albeit only one of a great many.

CHAPTER 9

Iron Chink Smith

Most people said it could never be done. The Chinese "slitters" hoped that it could not be done. Mr. Edward S. Deming, president and general manager of Pacific American Fisheries knew it could not be done. He was riding the street-car—undoubtedly for political reasons—in Fairhaven, Washington. When he heard a corpulent passenger tell the driver that he was inventing a machine that could grab the slimy fish, lop off the fins, split the belly, and remove the head, tail and entrails, he thought the fellow was demented. Anyone who had watched the swift swipes of the Chinese butchers knew that a machine could not improve on their work.

Of course Mr. E. A. Smith had never seen the inside of a cannery until a couple of years before when he had spent a day in the plant of E. B. Dudden on the Seattle waterfront. Since then he had come up with something he thought might work. He followed Mr. Deming into his office, introduced himself and proceeded to explain his Iron Chink to the incredulous president. A while later he left with permission to install two sample machines in their Bellingham plant and one in a cannery at Anacortes.

The first models of the Iron Chink were constantly in need of repair but Smith lived right at the cannery, sleeping between emergencies in a tattered canvas chair in the office. This way he soon learned what modifications had to be made. In 1906 the tubby Smith received his first cheque for an improved machine that could handle up to 80 fish per minute and in the same year models were sold on the Canadian coast.

E. A. Smith was an Ontario Canadian with a round, jovial face and at least three chins. He was a cook by trade, an inveterate humourist and practical joker by nature, and an inventive genius whose success ushered a new era into the fishing industry but whose life, so full of laughter, ended in pathos.

Smith had seen hard times, but before gaining security through his inventions, he applied his genius to scheming and thus always managed to emerge from adverse circumstances a little the *better* for wear. At one time he was running a cook-house in Cascade, B.C. Business was slack and Smith knew that something had to be done or he would have to pack up and leave town. The results of his concentration actually served to hasten his departure though it did alleviate his financial problem for awhile.

He suddenly became a public spirited personality and invited the townsfolk to join him in subscribing for prizes to be given at a community sports day. Just to show his magnanimity he donated the first $50. The money came rolling in till on the day of the races well over $500 was in the kitty. No one knew exactly why $300 of it was designed for the "Fat-man's" race. Just the same, no one worried when they saw the ponderous Smith waddle over to the starting line. He was by far the heaviest contestant and there was no danger that such a load of flesh could ever propel itself with enough velocity to win a race.

The starting flag dropped. Down the main street thundered the little herd of heavy-weights, puffing and wheezing through a cloud of dust. With eyes bulging like startled steers they crossed the finish line, heaving frightfully and pouring sweat. Bringing up the rear amid roars of laughter from the folk gathered along the side, waddled E. A. Smith, shaking like a jelly.

"I win! I win!" he gasped as he dragged across the finish line. There were more howls of laughter. But while everyone was wiping away tears of merriment and lighting fresh cigars, Smith was pointing out to the judges the fine print on the rules which he had drawn up himself and submitted to the printer. There it was, sure enough! No one would be eligible for the prize in the fat man's race unless over 280 pounds.

One by one the contestants weighed in. The first to cross the line was a mere 250 lbs., the next was not much more. In fact it was soon discovered that the only one to qualify was Mr. Smith at 320 lbs. He collected the money, but barely escaped with his life.

Smith had learned to manipulate circumstances to his own benefit out of sheer necessity for he had been poor most of his life. Travelling on the night boat between Portland and Bellingham he would purchase a ticket for an upper berth at $1.50 rather than the lower at $2.00. Then he would stroll around the decks. When his cabin-mate was ready to pop into bed Smith would enter the cabin. Passing the usual cordialities, he would grab the upper berth and shake it violently, punch it with the heel of his fist and wagging his head with a dismayed expression, examine the corners and the joints.

"What the Hell are you doing that for?" the bewildered passenger would ask.

"O it's pretty embarrassing to be this heavy," Smith would reply with a burdened sigh. "They simply don't make these contraptions strong enough. The last time the fellow below . . ." Here his voice would trail off. "But this one might be all right. We'll soon find out—ha! ha!—won't we?" He would chuckle and begin to unbutton his shirt. If any more persuasion was needed he would suddenly stop in the middle of undressing and stare at a vital spot on the bunk as though having made a new discovery, then shaking the thing as hard as possible he would deplore the poor construction that went into such objects. By this time his cabin mate would be insisting on taking the upper bunk in spite of Smith's feeble protests.

In 1909 E. A. Smith, now a financial success, confided to Mr. Deming who had become his good friend, "I've lived on skimmed milk all my life. Now I'm going to taste the cream."

He was going to escort his sister to the Seattle Fair and see everything there was to see no matter what the cost. He did. But on the return journey he backed his car into a boulder and the gas tank exploded, enveloping the vehicle in flames. Smith managed to get his sister out of the car and dragged to safety but in the process he was badly burned. In hospital he forced a smile and said to the doctor, "Doc, if you can just save a finger and a thumb on one hand I'll be satisfied." But Iron Chink Smith died two days later.

His invention revolutionized the industry. An Iron Chink on a pack of 800 cases eliminated six slitters at $2.50 per day, and saved up to half a salmon per case in the cutting. Of course the machine was expensive at the outset. Bought through Smith Canning Machine Co. of Seattle (though manufactured at Victoria Machine Works) the Iron Chink in the early days sold for $3,900, or could be rented for $1,500.00 cash and 5c per case on a minimum pack of 30,000 cases. Soon no operation could afford to be without one.

Other innovations and mechanical improvements impinged upon the operators. The old method of producing a vacuum was to punch a hole in the hot can. Juice and steam would squirt eight to twelve feet in the air. Then before the can cooled a drop of solder was placed over the hole. This primitive system was eliminated by the invention of exhaust boxes and eventually highly sophisticated vacuum chamber machines.

Manufactured cans were purchased eliminating the laborious process of making them by hand, and eventually the persistence of a Mr. John Young of the American Can Co. resulted in a method of collapsing the cans for shipment and reforming them on a "reform" machine, so that a case that ordinarily held forty-eight cans, empty or full, could now carry 330 collapsed can bodies. The old process of rolling the ends of the cans through a narrow trough of molten solder gave way to fast, efficient crimping machines. Even the filling of the cans could be done mechanically. But all this meant expensive additions to the plants, many of which were not well laid out for the new processes.

Consequently, the difficulties imposed by the big runs of 1897 and 1901, the growing power of a belligerent labour union movement and the capital cost of technical improvements such as Smith's Iron Chink meant that numerous small outfits could not survive. Some form of amalgamation was inevitable.

CHAPTER **10**

The Amalgamators

If Henry Ogle Bell-Irving could have had the least premonition of what was about to happen he would never have started out on the fifty mile hike over the old Cariboo Trail. He would have packed his belongings and headed back to Dumfriesshire in Scotland.

He had received his basic education at Merchiston school in Edinburgh before going to Carlsruhe in Germany, where he graduated in Engineering. In England he practiced his profession for four years, then boarded the *"Rolling Polly"* and sailed for Canada to work as a surveying engineer on the building of the C.P.R. west of Winnipeg. When the crew reached Salmon Arm, B.C., he decided to hike over the trail and meet the gang working east from Vancouver under H. Cambie. This is when it happened.

Half-way along the tortuous trail, knapsack piled high, tripod slung over one shoulder, Henry was plodding along when a handful of dishevelled looking fellows ambled out of the bush and approached him. He felt a little uneasy as they drew near, but was taken completely by surprise when he was suddenly struck to the ground. They robbed him of everything except the surveying instruments. It was with these as his sole possessions that he landed in Granville in the Fall of 1885, at the age of twenty-nine.

Within a year the young engineer had saved enough to go back to England, marry his sweetheart, and return with her to the new city on the coast. It was a financial undertaking not so formidable as one might believe, for the fare was only $10 each owing to the gold rate war then raging.

Nothing could have been a better prospect for an energetic businessman than real estate following the fire that ravished Granville on June 13th, 1886, and Henry Bell-Irving was quick to see opportunity. Along with R. G. Tatlow, later to be Provincial Minister of Finance, he commenced a business that was to continue to this Centennial year.

But he was not content to limit himself to real estate. Vancouver, like a phoenix rising from the ashes, promised to supersede Victoria as the ocean harbour of the west. Bell-Irving foresaw this and entered the export-import business. In 1889 he chartered the 879 ton clipper *Titania,* which had won fame for swift passages in the China tea trade. With it he imported the first general cargo from London to Vancouver via the Horn and among the important items of the bill of lading was a quantity of good Scotch whisky at 3s 4d per gallon and almost as much gin at 2s 11d per gallon, certainly prime necessities for a frontier city. On the return trip he sent the *Titania* full of B.C. canned sockeye salmon. It was this experience of gathering up a full shipment for export that interested him in the canning industry.

The thing that impressed him was the fact that he had to collect the full shipment from so many different canneries. He realized the difficulties experienced by the smaller outfits, knew that it was a waste of capital to have so many individual plants running in competition. He was present at the ceremony marking the completion of the Canadian Pacific Railway into Vancouver on 23rd May, 1887, and with the expansion of Vancouver as a harbour he could see possibilities for the formation of a large, strong company that could withstand the growing pressures by consolidation and at the same time take advantage of expanding market possibilities.

Efforts had been made in the past to form a combination. A

Mr. Fred Wheeler, Vancouver representative of the Great Northern Railway Company, had failed to get the idea accepted a few years earlier. But Henry Bell-Irving was both persistent and persuasive. He called on practically all the canners and cited the example of the Alaska Packers Association which had taken in fourteen canneries. He spoke of the growing threat of American traps on Puget Sound cutting into the runs, the need to counteract the over-expansion tendencies on the Canadian scene. After months of negotiating he finally managed to secure options on nine canneries. He returned to England in 1891 where, with the aid of influential friends and through the sale of 20,000 shares, the necessary capital was raised. Thus was formed one of the most highly esteemed companies on the coast, and at the time of formation the largest producer of Pacific salmon in the world: the Anglo-British Columbia Packing Co. Ltd. The Vancouver Agent, naturally, was the Bell-Irving Company.

Henry Ogle Bell-Irving was a remarkable man. High principled, sensitive, artistic yet practical and astute in business, he founded a strong company, a fine family tradition and at the same time worked towards the long range well-being and preservation of the industry even if it meant foregoing attractive, immediate gains. He was the first to realize the importance of independent inspection of processed fish and was an early advocate of more strict regulations governing the exploitation of the runs. An avid photographer and gifted artist, he would wander off into the hinterland to paint or take pictures and at the same time make notes of the spawning beds and conditions on the streams. With the aid of these he was able to speak authoritatively on the need for conservation. He was among the first to agitate for joint Canadian and American control of Fraser River fish and he became a very prominent civic figure in a rapidly growing Vancouver.

A lover of sports and the outdoors, he was a keen yachtsman, a big-game hunter, and up to the time of his death at the age of seventy-six was still figure skating. He was in fact another example of the high calibre of man that characterized much of the fishing industry.

Those who ventured out onto temperamental waters in skinny boats, huddling over their Swede stoves, nursing a mug of black coffee in the bleak, dawn hours were men of independent spirit, great courage and persevering will. But the men who took economic risks and who dared to steer a course of business through the turbulent conditions that have always prevailed in the fishing industry, were also courageous, and economically more daring than the men in the boats. Henry Ogle Bell-Irving was one of the finest. He was not a pioneer strictly speaking, for the industry was well under way by the time of his arrival. Yet his formation of the A.B.C. Company paved the way for other amalgamations which were to transform commercial salmon fishing.

Not all the amalgamations were successful. Shortly after the A.B.C. Company was formed, for example, the canneries for which Rithet and Co. were agents united into the Victoria Canning Company. The new combine also acquired Cascade Cannery on the Nass River and the fishing privileges in Quashela Lagoon on Smith's Inlet. But the company failed to show the anticipated profits and it was consequently swallowed up in the greatest amalgamation of them all; the British Columbia Packers Association.

Henry Doyle was only twenty-seven when he engineered the formation of British Columbia Packers' Association. His father had opened the first fishing supplies business in San Francisco back in 1875 only ten years after the start of salmon canning on the Pacific coast and at a time when San Francisco was the Mecca to which operators from there to Alaska retired annually. So young Henry grew up amid the cigar smoke and tobacco juice of these hardy gentlemen who all knew his father.

Henry turned out to be a very aggressive businessman. He could be quite vitriolic and was a scathing critic of those who were not blessed with the same opinion as himself. Yet he was assiduous in business, keeping detailed notes on catches and other aspects of the operation of numerous companies throughout most of his career, and he was as determined as a mountain goat in striving to attain his ambitions.

On April 8th, 1902, with the approval of the bank and the financial backing of Aemelius Jervis and Co. in Toronto, this young man succeeded in forming a company that purchased twenty-nine out of the forty-eight plants on the Fraser and another twelve up-coast, at a cost of $931,641.11 cash and 1,496,560 shares in stock. Appropriately enough, the first president was Alexander Ewen, the first general manager, Henry Doyle.

Bringing his idea to fruition was not all plain sailing as the following incident attests. All through the Fall of 1901 Doyle worked out his plan for amalgamation. Early in the new year he got recommendations from local banks and went East to the head offices where he secured backing and where in the space of two weeks with the aid of Jervis he had organized a syndicate to furnish the capital.

The banks were to put at his disposal the cash underwritten by the syndicate. These funds were to be forwarded through the local Vancouver branch. However when Doyle and the syndicate's representative went to the local bank manager to make sure the funds were on hand they discovered that nothing had been done. The manager shifted uncomfortably in his chair and suggested that since he was being put to considerable inconvenience in the whole affair he could see no reason for proceeding until his personal services had been adequately recognized. It was preposterous, he admitted with an uneasy smile, but after all everybody had to look out for himself and he was confident that his request would be easily met by so powerful an enterprise.

While he was talking the representative from the east was scribbling on a piece of paper. He handed it to the manager and said, "Unless that money is here by 10 o'clock tomorrow morning this wire goes to your head office." The wire read, "Our work has been completed as agreed upon. We are ready to take up our options and pay what cash they call for, but the manager of the bank here declines to honour your instructions to him and your pledge to us until we agree to pay him an honorarium not earned. Advise me at once."[1] The money was available next morning!

Sometimes Doyle was amazed at what he discovered travelling from cannery to cannery securing options. At Alert Bay a salmon saltery had been established in 1862 by Mack and Neill. Then in 1881 S. A. Spencer and T. Earle built there the first cannery to be erected on the coast outside of the Skeena and Fraser rivers. It was built to exploit the sockeye run to the Nimpkish River. But it took a special kind of management, for the Indians of the area, not yet seduced by the white man's voracious standards of economics would quit fishing when they felt that they had enough to give them food for the winter and credit from the cannery store. Stephen Spencer was one of the few people who in those early days could induce them to continue fishing when he needed more fish, and when he failed, he was wise enough to be content with what he did get.

Although he had been a photographer in Victoria for some years, he was much happier living with the Nimpkish people all year round. There was little in Alert Bay to induce anyone to remain once the fishing was over, but this backwoods character was happy there, and every year he managed to ship out a sizable load of canned salmon. When negotiating a price for the business, Doyle asked if he could see the books so that he would be better able to assess the value of the operation.

"The what?" replied Spencer.

"The books — you know, the records of your income and expe . . ."

"Oh, those," cut in the rugged old canner. "I never keep books."

Doyle was flabbergasted. "But how do you run a business without keeping records?" he enquired, thinking that perhaps the old fellow was hedging.

"All I know is that every year there is about $10,000 more in my bank account than there was the year before. You can ask the manager. And if you still don't believe it, I can easily keep the property."

B.C. Packers Association bought the property in 1902 — without seeing the books.

Doyle resigned only two years after the new venture he had worked so hard to instigate had been operating. Stories vary as to the cause. Certainly there was disagreement over shifting the insurance to Eastern companies, and even Alex Ewen resigned due to the controversy over failing to fill positions with previous cannery owners. But the thing that hurt Henry Doyle most of all was the accusation that he as general manager had shown incompetence by thrusting the Association into over-expansion.

Doyle severed his immediate relationship with the company he had helped form, but his name was not to be easily eradicated from the fishing industry. For years he was involved in the acquisition and disposal of some of the most prominent canneries on the coast, and for a while he and names like the Wallace Brothers, Captain R. E. Gosse, Francis Millerd, Dawson and Buttimer, and R. V. Wrinch were competitive thorns in the side of that young giant, B.C. Packers Association.

To list the shuffle of properties, to enumerate the purchases and trades, the burning, dismantling, foreclosing, selling, relocating and building, and to mention a fraction of the names involved, would be to present a piece of reading as formidable as any student of the subject would want to encounter. The years following 1901 were years of robust competition when the industry spread up-coast in search of wealth. No longer could they afford to ignore the coarser species of salmon. Cohoe, pinks and chums were fished as avariciously as the sockeye. The wildness of the northern coast transferred something of itself to the beings who fished and canned. Dare-devil piracy of nets was not unknown, ignoring regulations and robbing creeks was common practice. The canneries had to have fish and frantic operators armed with a small navy of testy fishermen carried on business that was sometimes more akin to war.

The coast was cluttered with canneries. In 1901 forty-seven companies operated seventy-three plants, many of them stark, unpainted plank-buildings that clung to the shore in some obscure inlet. By 1914 there were seventy-seven operating plants, though in the interim a number had been destroyed by fire. Three years later the number had jumped to ninety-four. Something had to give.

Faster transportation, improved canning techniques involving greater capital outlay, threatening extinction of major runs of salmon and more strict government control made the small operational unit impractical. Outfits like Anglo-British Columbia Packers and British Columbia Packers Association with canneries scattered from Skeena to Fraser found it more economical to bring the fish to one or two centrally located canneries and to leave the others idle.

Other firms were to enter the field, strong firms like the Canadian Fishing Company which was primarily interested in halibut and fresh salmon but which built the first cannery in Vancouver city in 1918 and went on to become one of the leaders of the industry, purchasing and building a score of canneries as well as freezing and cold storage plants. In 1929 dissatisfaction among trollers of the west coast of Vancouver Island led to a co-operative marketing venture, the beginning of a movement that culminated in one of the finest enterprises in the country, the Prince Rupert Fishermen's Co-operative Association. There came the Nelson brothers, Richard and Norman, who specialized in salting herring and salmon and eventually, as late as 1932, entered the canning business with their famous St. Mungo cannery on the Fraser. Even some small outfits managed to maintain equilibrium because of strong family traditions of leadership and careful management. For example, Cassiar Packing Co. on the Skeena slough commenced canning in 1903. Today it is operated by the grandson of Alexander Ewen. Todd and Sons weathered the storms because of wisely invested wealth and after amalgamating with B.C. Packers in 1928 Francis Millerd slipped back into business and has held on tenaciously ever since.

Nevertheless the heyday of canning was over by the end of World War I. Eventually even some of the most stable of the independent operators succumbed to the temptation and sold out to one of the "big four", B.C. Packers, Canadian Fish, Anglo-B.C. Packers or Nelson Brothers. Sometimes the finale of a career was tinged with pathos, — as in the case of John Wallace.

John and Peter Wallace were independent Scotsmen who settled in the Columbia River district where they established a fresh fish business that shipped the first fresh salmon across the continent to New York. Their main interest, however, was sturgeon and when the Columbia supply dwindled due to overfishing, they moved to the Fraser. But the mighty sturgeon, weighing as much as six, seven or even nine hundred pounds, could not withstand the onslaught of commercial exploitation and soon their numbers were negligible. The Wallaces moved into salmon canning and, separately and together, hewed out a considerable empire which included control of such well-known canneries as Claxton on the Skeena, Arrandale on the Nass, Butedale on Princess Royal Island, Kildonan on Vancouver Island, Strathcona on Rivers Inlet and Hickey on Smiths Inlet.

At last, in middle age and able to afford a few of the luxuries which he had not enjoyed in earlier life, John Wallace decided that he would take a trip to his homeland. He got as far as Liverpool, disembarked from the liner and died on the dock.

Another story with a tragic ending is that of George W. Dawson and Fred J. Buttimer, who as well as being partners were brothers-in-law. But here the similarities ended, for these New Brunswickers were as different as the raven from the seagull. Buttimer was short, mild mannered, retiring and quiet, though a shrewd judge in business. Dawson was large, very distinguished looking, usually silent, but beset with a stormy temper that could be triggered by the slightest provocation and which erupted into violence that was not always limited to speech. Nor did he get over a grudge easily.

Once while travelling with a friend in the smoking compartment of the interurban tram line that ran between Vancouver and New Westminster, Dawson got so excited and angered while simply relating an incident, that he was waving his fist under his friend's nose in a most menacing manner and some of the other passengers, who could see the action through the glass partition but could not hear the conversation, jumped up in alarm ready to defend the threatened passenger. On another occasion Henry Doyle brought a paper for him to sign and almost got kicked out of the office before he had an opportunity to explain fully what it was.

The reason for the outburst went back a few years. After selling their Brunswick plants to B.C. Packers Association, Dawson and Buttimer built a small cannery on Harlock Island in 1905. They had no boats now, so they engaged a fellow by the name of Perry Rogers with his boat the *Lapwing* to buy fish from the fleet at the mouth of the river. Until this time the fishermen were obliged to deliver their fish to a particular cannery either because they leased the boat and net from that cannery, or because they were bound by contract or financial obligation. When Perry Rogers took fish and paid cash out on the grounds, immediately the incensed Fraser River Canners Association filed a lawsuit against Dawson and Buttimer. They were acquitted, thus breaking forever the legal chains by which operators held claim to a fisherman's entire catch, but Dawson never forgot the incident and remained bitter toward the member operators. It was a bitterness which poisoned his personality and for which even time could effect no antidote.

This was the underlying reason for his rage when Doyle presented him with the document to sign. The Fraser River Canners' Association had changed its name to the British Columbia Canners' Association in order to include the northern plants, one of their main motives being a need for additional revenue. But many of the northern operators did not belong and they decided to draw up a memorial pointing out that the association did not speak for the whole industry, and that should legislation be pending, the government ought not to be guided in judgment by the overtures of this body alone, but ought also to hear from the other canners.

Doyle was asking Dawson to sign this memorial, but at the very sound of the name he flew into a rage that lasted a full five minutes. He threw the document on the floor and kicked it half way across the room. He pounded on the desk, flailed his arms, spluttered out a stream of profanities which he regretted were too mild to describe what he thought of the Association until finally, during a lull, when he was catching breath for the second instalment of the outburst, Doyle explained that the memorial was drawn up by those *not* belonging to the Association. Dawson looked at him for a long time. Then he slowly crossed the room, picked up the paper, returned to his desk and signed it.

"Perhaps I better keep this for a few days," he said. "I'm sure I can get a few more signatures on it for you. That way it will carry more weight."

Dawson regarded his ungovernable temper as an affliction, something he deeply regretted but was powerless to control. He was unpopular with the other operators, which was in itself tragic, for the men who canned salmon on the coast formed a unique fraternity. Perhaps this was because the obstacles they faced in common were greater than the threat they presented to one another as competitors. Dawson, however, did not share in this fellowship.

He had one deep friendship, and that was with his brother. During the winter months when the canneries were silent and still, Sam and George Dawson could be seen every day walking home at lunch-time to the cottage at the corner of Hastings and Westminster Avenue (now Main Street) and it was said that you could set your watch by their regularity. At the end of the day too, with slow, measured step and looking straight ahead, the brothers could be seen wending their way home. Then Sam died, and George Dawson was never seen taking the same route again.

Shortly after this the long and successful association of Dawson and Buttimer ended in anger. True to his nature Dawson festered with vindictive hostility towards his brother-in-law and let it be known that the crowning joy of his life would be to gloat over the grave of Buttimer. It was not long till he *was* at the funeral of his old partner. But he was a downcast, lonely and broken man. He had achieved wealth but lost the richest treasure of all — friendship.

It was in 1924 that Dawson and Buttimer sold out to Canadian Fishing Company Limited. Like most of their contemporaries their canneries at Kildala, Rivers Inlet and Manitou on Dean Channel were eventually used as fish camps or abandoned completely. By 1942 only thirty operating canneries were left on the coast.

British Columbia Packers Association more than any other was responsible for the absorption of the numerous plants that used to fill the inlets with their stench and steam. In 1914 the Association was incorporated as British Columbia Fishing and Packing Co. Limited and in 1928 the name was changed to B.C. Packers Limited. Throughout the growth of this company scores of canneries were devoured. Often they were purchased and immediately boarded up, never again to vibrate with the pulse of production. When H. R. MacMillan became president in 1933 he waded in with the same dynamic business genius for which he was renowned in other fields, and through diversification B.C. Packers came to enjoy a degree of health which had not been characteristic of their own firm nor of the industry at large.

Today you may travel the long lonely inlets and see the scars of yesteryear's activity, mere blemishes on the beaches, a few gaunt pilings protruding from the water of a quiet bay, the lighter green of new growth on the shore, a barnacle-clad boiler tilted in the tide. There is a strange silence about these tiny wastelands and a sad nostalgia seeps into the senses as you try to visualize the life that used to be there.

CHAPTER **11**

The Price of Fish

Ordinarily when Vic Erickson went to Vancouver he drank every last penny he had made at hand-logging, trapping and fishing during the previous year. A few weeks of wild drinking and fighting and he would end up in a cheap skid-row hotel hung-over, sick and broke. Then he would climb aboard his little troller, crank up the engine, and head back up-coast. Not until the last faint shadow of Point Grey faded behind him would his spirit be put at ease. That is how it usually was. But not this time. This trip he really did buy the new boat that he had talked about so often, though he never got it home.

It had been a good winter for furs. Even his own trap line had produced well, though Erickson never confined himself to his own line if he thought he could get away with a little poaching. He was a short wiry man with huge, powerful hands in which he could pick a mink out of a trap and with one squeeze stop its heart. He feared neither man nor nature and even in winter when the weather was mean and unpredictable, he could be seen setting out from Duncanby Landing in a small row boat, pulling against the waves to go and check his trap line.

He was a tough man and everybody on the Inlet knew it, though Jessie Graham also knew that he had a touch of tenderness. Jessie and Jimmy Graham owned and operated the store and marine facilities at Duncanby, a bright splash of red and white painted buildings set against the drab green of the forested hills and rocky outcroppings. Here the fishermen and trappers could tie up at the floats, buy grub at the store, mend their nets and boats, and most important, drink Hudson's Bay rum, talk and spit at the water. Jessie and Jimmy were great friends of all fishermen, a few of whom like Vic Erickson lived on their boats all winter tied up inside the floats.

One day when Vic was sharpening his knife Jessie offered to help him by turning the grindstone.

"Here, let me turn the wheel," she said, "you can't hold the knife and turn at the same time."

Vic looked at her with a sort of puzzled frown that gradually spread into a smile of pleasure as he applied the knife while Jessie turned the handle. Each time he straightened up from the wheel to rub his thumb across the blade he looked at Jessie and said,

"Ja know Jessie, I'm gonna tell ja, yer jhust like my ol mother — sorta remind me of her — seeing ja standing thar — turnin' that wheel." He put the blade to the stone again. "Jah by gee — jhust the way ya looked a minute ago — turnin' the handle."

There was a long pause in the conversation while Vic seemed to concentrate on getting an edge on the knife. Jessie thought he had ended the subject when he suddenly broke in.

"My mother used to be a virry relijouce woman, you know." Another long pause followed. More feeling the edge. More grinding.

"Yes indeed — verrry relijouce. Very relijouce indeed." Still the grinding went on.

"O she was relijouce all right — but she couldn't help it — and she was a good woman just the same."

Jessie looked at him. He was perfectly serious. Somewhere in the memory of this hardened, battered man there was the picture of a good woman — in spite of her religion.

When spring began to seep into the mists of the inlet, Erickson rigged up his trolling poles and headed out to the surf line on the other side of Calvert Island. All summer long he dragged his flashing lures, hooking the hungry Springs and Cohoes, icing them down for delivery, salting away his money. It was hard work with long hours of monotony when the fish were not striking. But Vic Erickson was as seasoned as the planking of his deck, and each time he ran to Port John with a load, he would count his money and think about the new boat. By fall he had enough money and he headed for town to find himself the vessel he wanted. He went directly to a boat builder and made the purchase before he could spend the cash on a bender.

It was near Christmas by the time everything was straightened out and he was anxious to get out of Vancouver. He never felt good in town. The city was no place to be at Christmas time in any case. Back at Duncanby the Grahams would have a few of the boys in and everything would be nice and homelike. Up on the inlet, a fellow knew who he was, not like in the city. He could hardly wait to see their faces when he would pull in and tie up the new boat at the floats. He decided to head back right away. Besides, some bastard might be poaching his trap line. He had to get back.

It was a dirty afternoon when he left Cascade harbour that December, but Vic Erickson had been in lots of sloppy weather and with the new boat he knew he could take quite a lot of sea. Anyway his mind was made up, and once that happened it took a lot to stop him.

But Vic Erickson did not reach Duncanby. He disappeared and was never heard from again. Not a trace of the brand new boat, nor of Vic, was ever found.

Change the name, the time, the place and you have the story of hundreds of hardy men who have wrestled with nature, plucking from her the wealth of her waters and shorelines, waiting out her tantrums, now and then defying her, but finally succumbing to her power. Every year, even today when the fishing fleet is made up of sturdier boats with radio phones and high-powered engines, the season takes its toll of lives. A stalled engine and the vessel drifts onto a reef, a propeller wrapped in fishnet renders the boat powerless so that she is driven ashore, a plank springs on an old vessel in heavy seas, a leaky gas-line, a cigarette and an explosion, a fatigued fisherman falls asleep at the wheel and ploughs into a rock, splitting the bow stem, a sudden gust of wind or a wicked rip-tide and the boat turns over — always the fisherman is in peril. Though many are rescued from watery ordeals, many others go down.

In earlier days the dangers were multiplied, the discomforts oppressive. On Sunday afternoon the cannery steamer could be seen pulling out from the wharf towing a score or more fishing skiffs, each one containing two men, a "puller" to handle the oars, and the fisherman to handle the linen net. A chunk of patchy canvas that doubled as a sail was stretched across the boom to provide shelter against the wind, the spray and the rain.

Soon one boat after another would veer off from the wake of the steamer. The rudder was set, the painter slipped through the ring spliced onto the towline, the sail was hoisted and the gill-netter manoeuvered by oar and sail, ready to set the net as soon as the six o'clock cannon went off.

All night long they drifted with their nets, the yellow glow of lanterns and stoves splashing on the murky darkness like a million dancing fireflies. In big years as many as three thousand boats crammed the Fraser. From Mission City fifty miles upstream, to the mouth of both north and south arms that hug Lulu Island, the flat-bottom skiffs were scattered in what appeared to be, and often was, sheer confusion. Spilling out of the mouth where the stained water of the river spread into the blue of Georgia Straits the double-ended Columbia River boats fought the tides. Up on Skeena and Rivers Inlet it was the same.

By five o'clock in the morning the fleet had drifted miles with the tide. Some would be bracing themselves with black coffee against the bleak morning, some would be hauling in their nets. Others would have their sails up, or would be rowing hard against the current to get back into position for another drift. Around the mouth those who had drifted far out onto the open were towed back to the muddy water where fishing was better during daylight.

Beneath the canvas wrapped in oil-skin was a man's grub — a loaf of bread that was soon soggy in spite of the oilskin, a few hardtack biscuits, a can of coffee and his tobacco. With these and the dismal comfort of his stove, probably nothing more than an old, four-gallon oil can with the end cut out and a hole near the bottom for draught, the fisherman and his partner stayed out on the grounds for the better part of a week. Wet with incessant rain, scorched by the sun, chilled in the morning mists, legs cramped, hands cracked and smarting from the saltwater and fish-slime, they were at the mercy of nature's whims.

Gradually some of the harshness was eliminated through invention. When "Swede" stoves that burned coal-oil were made available they were considered a great luxury. Over it the fisherman could boil his coffee, or even fry an egg if he were really ambitious. The cramped "dog-house" that became standard structure on gillnetters for many years, kept a man out of the worst of the wind and rain even if he could barely turn around once inside. Eventually legislation prohibiting the use of powered boats in salmon fishing was overcome and in the early twenties, in spite of the obdurate opinions of people in Ottawa who had never seen a fishing boat, the puller was replaced by the one lung "Easthope" — the workhorse of the sea — and its rival the "Vivian." But even the sturdiest boat and the strongest engine becomes a mere plaything in the fingers of the sea when her fury is aroused.

If a storm came up suddenly the fleet was scattered and in spite of efforts to find them and tow them to safety the cannery steamers were often forced to abandon the search, knowing full well that the calm would bring with it the grim statistics of tragedy.

On July 23, 1898, some two thousand gillnetters were fishing around the mouth of the Fraser when a storm sprang up. Boats were hurled together and crunched like eggshells. Others were swamped with one crashing wave. Some were blown out to sea never to be seen again. By the next day twenty-two fishermen were lost, most of them Canadian Japanese from the settlement at Steveston.

Sometimes a tragedy or near tragedy occurred, not so much on account of the caprice of the ocean but because of foolhardiness and ignorance on the part of those who dared to tangle with her. Perhaps more have been drowned by booze than by salt water.

Every now and then a few gallant adventurers who have read or heard about the fabulous catches of salmon on the coast and who are equipped with a greater degree of greed than good sense, find themselves afloat in a fishing boat before they realize what they have done. Once a group of boys from Okotoks, Alberta, rented out their farms and came to Prince Rupert where they succeeded in getting a boat and some equipment, and set out in search of fish. It was two weeks before they were found, near Bella Bella two hundred miles south, without a fish in the hold, the net in ribbons, half starved, and several thousand dollars in debt.

Sometimes it is a grim battle between two inexorable forces, the sea with all its might and a salty fisherman with craft and knowledge, stamina and nerve as his weapons. Such was the case of Ken Campbell.

Campbell was a dour, independent Scot who was about as familiar a landmark up-coast as some of the rocks. He had fished many seasons and had developed that economy of words and work that makes old men more durable than many an energetic youth. He knew the tides like a commuter knows a bus schedule, and a glance at the evening sky told him how to prepare for tomorrow. Most of his life had been spent in contest with the elements never in foolhardy risks or daredevil stunts, but the sagacious judging of what might be safely done under the prevailing temper of sea and wind. Even when he pulled out into the fog that June seventh, back in 1958, it was not his misjudgment of the weather that got him into trouble.

He was headed for Port Hardy at the north end of Vancouver Island, a trip he had often made from Duncanby in about ten hours. The *Betty,* his thirty-two foot troller and gillnetter was like himself, a little old and slow but sturdy and reliable, and even though quite a few fishermen were moving to faster, more high-powered engines, Ken Campbell liked the "Easthope." It was an engine that had a good reputation for dependability. Furthermore he knew every nut and bolt in it and claimed that he could keep it running just on the smell of gasoline. He was not alarmed therefore, when several hours out the engine spluttered a few times, coughed and died.

How often he had improvised with wire and tape and managed to limp into harbour. How often he had found the water pump jammed with seaweed or the distributor cap cracked, the gas line plugged or a valve sticking, yet managed to repair the damage at least long enough to get to a camp or a cannery where he could work on it or replace a part if necessary. But this time, for some reason or other, he was unable to locate the trouble right away.

He had been working methodically for several hours, checking out one possibility after another, when he became aware that the wind was stronger and the ground swells were rising. He climbed out onto deck and was surprised to discover how far off shore he had drifted. The fog had been swept away by the developing south-easterner that was driving him farther and farther out to sea.

Already the mountains of the mainland were diminished to a faint ragged hedge on the horizon. Much farther and he would be completely out of sight of passing coastal vessels and the chance of being picked up would be slim indeed. He opened his can of sealed flares and lit one, though after it had burned out he knew it was futile and decided to wait till he could see a ship before lighting another. No sense wasting them.

It was impossible to work on the engine now. Mountains of water raced in upon the tiny craft. One moment he was in the trough with a wave hanging menacingly above, the following instant the boat hovered on the summit of a swell before sliding with a sickening sensation into the next trough. The little troller pitched and reeled violently and every wave threatened to be the last.

In an effort to keep the bow into the swells, he rigged up a sea-anchor by tying everything that was loose onto the anchor line and dropping it overboard. The violent lurching snapped the stabilizer poles and as darkness descended upon him, Campbell had little hope of lasting through the night. One wave taken at the wrong moment, and he knew it would be the end. Questions kept racing through his mind. Would the caulking hold? Would a plank spring in the merciless pounding? Would a sudden gust of wind lay him over? Slowly the hours dragged on while Campbell held on to keep himself from being knocked about inside the cabin. When dawn came the wind showed no sign of abating, and not a trace of land could be seen.

For six days Ken Campbell drifted, driven before the pitiless wind, battered by the swells. On the sixth day the wind died and the sea began to even out enough for him to resume work on the engine.

If he failed to get it going again there was no telling when, if ever, he would be picked up, for he had no idea how far off shore he had drifted. In every direction there was nothing to be seen but the undulating ocean.

Then another thought occurred. He had not bothered to "grub-up" heavily at Duncanby, expecting to be at Port Hardy within a matter of hours. About all he had left in the way of food were a few cans of beans and some coffee. He decided to ration himself to half a can of beans a day.

It was several hours before he managed to get a strong spark going to the plugs and when he spat on his grimy hands and grabbed the flywheel he hesitated for a moment. If he had been a praying man this would have been the moment. But Ken Campbell was not given to religion. He depended upon his own skills, so when the old Easthope spat and spun into rhythm he straightened up with a wry smile and a sense of satisfaction that belonged only to himself. Into the wheel-house he climbed and swung the bow due East. Sooner or later he had to come to land.

For two days the *Betty* churned over the backs of the ground swells. For two days old Campbell forced himself to keep awake, pointing the bow unerringly eastward, and on the second day the horizon began to take shape. Ever so faintly at first, then unmistakably the distant mountain peaks broke the surface of the sea. He was just beginning to feel a sense of relief when the regular rhythm of the engine was broken. For a few strokes it was all right, then it missed again and with a desperate gasping noise the old Easthope hissed to a stop.

He knew the trouble without even bothering to look. For the past few hours he had been wondering how long the gas would last. Now he knew that the tank was empty. Even checking with the dip stick was a futile gesture born out of habit. At the same time he realized that he had just made a mistake for which he would probably pay later. There was nothing to be done now but wait. Campbell flopped onto his narrow bunk, exhausted.

Perhaps it was the plunging of the boat that awoke him, but when he staggered out onto deck some time later the shore was plainly visible. The crow's feet about his eyes tightened as he scanned to recognize the place. He knew most of the coast from the Fraser to the Nass, but what he saw now was unfamiliar. It was a wild deserted stretch of coast, fringed with the white of breakers as the swells split upon the rocks.

A stiffening nor'-wester had been driving him for the past hours, and now as the *Betty* was being borne in towards the rocks he knew his one great mistake. He ought to have saved a couple of inches of gas in the bottom of the tank for a time like this. With a few minutes running time he might have slipped into a sheltered cove at the last moment. Now he was powerless. All he could do was to watch his doom approach.

Methodically, without the least sign of panic, Campbell made his final preparations. He sealed some matches into a small jar and shoved it into his pocket. Then he climbed to the bow and prepared the anchor. There was just a chance that he would be lucky enough to hit a part of the beach where the anchor would hold.

Now the *Betty* was racing with the waves. Directly ahead lay an ugly reef, beyond it an open stretch of water, then the beach. Even when he let the anchor go he knew that there was little hope of it holding. He watched the line play out, saw it tighten as the hook grabbed. The *Betty* swung around on the line. Just then a giant swell lifted the little fishing boat. The anchor line snapped like cotton thread and the *Betty* was swept away and dashed like a toy upon the reef. The whole starboard side ripped open and the sea came in. Campbell jumped.

How he got to shore he would never be able to tell, but somehow he found himself cast up on the friendless beach. He was bruised, soaked and shivering with cold — but alive. As soon as he got his breath he started out in search of shelter.

Ken Campbell's first stroke of luck came when he discovered two tiny hunter's cabins not far from the wreck. The matches had got wet after all so he was unable to light a fire. Though exhausted he was afraid to lie down and sleep for fear of perishing with the cold. All night he walked around the cabin in an effort to keep warm. Next day at low tide he scrounged around the beach close to the wreck. He recovered a few tins of beans and took them back to the shack. For another week the stubborn old Scot eked out the days in his desolate refuge living off the beans.

It was Saturday, June 28, when John Sparlstra flew over Toleak Point, forty miles south of Cape Flattery in the State of Washington. He thought he saw something on the rocks and circled for a second look. Sure enough, it was a wreck, a small fishing vessel. He reported it to the U.S. Coast Guard at La Push and gave them the location. That day a crew of three from the Coast Guard station slipped between the rocks with their motor surf-boat and picked up a Robinson Crusoe-like creature with a thick Scots burr and a bristly beard. He was not a talkative man so it was a while before they learned that he had been lost for 21 days and that he was three hundred miles from his destination.

Had it not been for Ken Campbell's deliberate and somewhat obstinate nature, as well as his skill and knowledge as a seaman, it is unlikely he would have survived. Others not so fortunate, though perhaps equally skilful have simply disappeared as in the case of Vic Erickson, or they leave a trace of mysterious tragedy that plays on the imagination.

One fisherman lost on Queen Charlotte Sound was found almost a year later in a shack on Aristazabal Island, a hundred miles from where he was thought to have gone down. He was sitting on a chair slumped over a table, but the condition of his body showed that he had not been long dead. Only imagination can supply the details of his lonely, agonizing death by starvation.

Folk around Fitzhugh Sound recall the strange disappearance of Gregson and his son. The family — mother and father, two daughters and one grown-up son — lived in Safety Cove where they had been buying fish from independent fishermen (and any who wanted a fistful of cash for week-end booze). It was just before Christmas when father and son decided to take the boat around the end of Calvert Island to prospect for another campsite where they could put a scow to buy spring-trolled fish.

They never returned.

Back at the float-house the mother and two daughters were stranded all through the holiday season. It was after the New Year before a boat happened to pull into the cove. When a search was made they discovered where the Gregson's vessel had gone down, in Grief Bay. Close to the marker light at Cape Calvert the battered remains of the skiff were found.

There were signs that at least one of them had managed to get to a shore, for a few empty cans were scattered about where a small fire had been built and an axe lay close to what appeared to have been a crude shelter.

There are today fantastic stories of how they managed to climb ashore only to be torn to pieces by wolves, or that they were murdered by Indians and buried deep in the bush. But these are highly imaginative tales coddled in the minds of the credulous.

97

Most folks in the area simply accept the fact that what happened to the Gregsons will never be known, for they were never found.

For the fisherman and his family life is lived in rhythm with the tides and the tempers of the wind. Death is always lurking close at hand and every community that has a wharf has seen the solemn knot of oilskinned men and weeping women bear a limp form from the boats to the forlorn household where he used to live and belong. On the wall of many a coastal cottage will be found the mounted photograph of a lad lost at sea, and when a storm springs up tension sets in till every father, husband and son is safely tied up behind the breakwater.

The cannery operators risked capital and economic ruin. They were truly courageous men willing to gamble against odds in order to grasp at a fortune. But the fisherman risks his life for a few dollars worth of fish, and the cost to countless mothers, wives and sweethearts cannot be estimated in money.

CHAPTER **12**

Rivers Inlet

Canada's Pacific salmon fishing is spread all along the broken coastline from Alaska to Washington. In tiny bays and secluded inlets, along the wild shores of Vancouver Island's West Coast, tucked in narrow channels and clinging to the feet of precipitous mountains, shoddy little canneries have defied the violent wilderness and filched fortunes from the sighing tides. Few passages of water were safe from the merciless sifting of the seine nets or the strangling web of the gillnets. But because of their concentrated runs of sockeye three main areas predominated as centres of the industry: the Fraser River in the south, the Nass and Skeena Rivers in the north and Rivers and Smith Inlets halfway between. But there are no active canneries on Rivers Inlet now.

Once it seemed that every bay, every sheltered cove along the thirty-five mile neck of sea was crammed with a spluttering cannery and its satellite buildings. Now only the derelict remains of places like Provincial, R.I.C. (Rivers Inlet Cannery), Brunswick, Kildala and Greens serve to remind one of the rowdy days when Rivers Inlet, more than 200 miles north of Vancouver, was alive with seventeen plants.

In those days every cannery site was a hotchpotch of people. Scots and Swedes mended their nets together at the racks. Japanese fishermen, always resented by the majority of whites, insulated themselves against hostility with industry and exclusiveness. Whole families of Indians were crowded into rows of crummy shacks where the squalor for which they were blamed was virtually unavoidable. Off by itself stood China House, gaunt and ugly, crowded beyond imagination. Further back were the bunk houses for single white men and the painted cottages reserved for those with families. Appearing somewhat like a governor's dwelling in a jungle colony, the cannery manager's house commanded a view over its patch of green lawn, probably built at the cost of every spoonful of soil that could be scraped up within a half-mile radius. There might even be flowers spilling out of boxes and tubs.

A cannery was a conglomeration of buildings and boardwalks where for a few hectic weeks during the summer, while the lusty sockeye surged up the inlet, fishermen and cannery workers of a dozen races and creeds mingled in furious activity bent upon earning as much money as possible during the short season.

Apparently, for many of them, the determination to get and stay drunk for as long as possible was a commensurate, if not a primary urge. On week-ends when the fishermen were there the boardwalks resounded to the clomp of carousers' boots, and the night was rent with cat-calls and wolf howls. Cracked craniums and black eyes were prevalent Sunday conditions, and the fact that there were few really serious outbreaks of violence must be credited, in great measure, to the vigilance and courage of Arthur Stone, for many years the provincial fishery and police officer.

Arthur Stone had come out from England about 1901. When his family followed him five years later they lived adjacent to Green's cannery, halfway up the Inlet. One room on the main floor of their home was completely filled with two cages constructed of flat-iron. Into these Arthur would deposit disturbers of the peace until they had cooled off or until court could be held, if absolutely necessary.

Stone was not out to get convictions. The whole inlet was one large community where in spite of the influx of thousands of fishermen and workers, the regulars were well known to one another and a man was accepted with all his idiosyncracies so long as he did not become too unruly. It was Stone's job to see that a reasonable degree of law and order was maintained. He was not fanatical about it. He knew practically everyone on a first name basis and had his own way of avoiding serious difficulty. If someone fired up with liquor became obstreperous, Stone's philosophy was that a well aimed punch on the jaw could be excused provided the fellow was quiet for the rest of the night.

One time he devised a unique cure for a habitual rampager. He threw him into a retort for cooking salmon. When the fellow awoke next morning he was frantic, fearing that someone might turn on the steam and render him to a pulp. He was careful never to be caught causing trouble again.

One of the most colourful aspects of life around the canneries on Rivers Inlet was China House. In spring the Union steamship churned up the channel loaded with people and paraphernalia, and once the gang-plank dropped a cluster of Chinese stampeded ashore. They usually brought with them a small herd of pigs and a flock of scrawny chickens. Behind their shedlike bunkhouse the Orientals kept their animals. Most Sunday mornings the tender nerves of Saturday's carousers were jangled by the squeals of a stuck pig accompanied by the high-pitched excitement of Orientals. Only after the frantic beast had splashed back and forth in its own blood and kicked its last on the crimson ground would the excitement subside. Then, following the gruesome butchery one of the men would trudge proudly to the door of the manager's house and present his wife with a liberal chunk of warm, gory pork. It was an act of generosity and perhaps political expediency seldom appreciated as it ought to have been.

The Chinese were quite excitable. At one cannery the lacquer machine was being filled when something happened that nearly resulted in the loss of the whole building. The lacquer that kept the cans from rusting, and which had replaced the old habit of painting the cans by hand, was mixed with high test gasoline in order that it would dry rapidly once applied. One of the men was adding this high test gas to the hopper that fed into the machine when a Chinese worker decided to fill his lighter. The lighter slipped. It fell on the trigger, sparked, and immediately there was a resounding woosh and the place was on fire.

In one body the Chinese made for the door, yelling, screaming and wildly flailing their arms. So great was their panic that no one could get in to fight the flames, and because they were all clambering to get out at once the door was plugged with squealing bodies. Some of them actually had to be dragged through. Eventually a few of the men got at the fire and extinguished it.

Besides being excitable, the Chinese cannery workers were extremely superstitious, a characteristic which sometimes resulted in comedy but more often in cruelty and tragedy. Such was the case that occurred in July 1904, when Dr. Large was the medical missionary on the Inlet.

In 1897 the Methodist Church had sent a Dr. J. A. Jackson to the Indian Village of Bella Bella. He died before many months helping the Indians move their houses and belongings to a new site. In 1898 Dr. R. W. Large, who had been working among the Japanese people at Steveston, came up-coast and took over the work which included a summer branch hospital on the Inlet, built a few years earlier by a Dr. Bolton. Dr. Large was a devout Methodist, an able physician and surgeon and the friend of anyone in need regardless of religion, race or colour.

What he found when he answered a call for help that July on the Inlet, fortified his conviction that the Gospel (as preached by the Methodist Church) was the only antidote for the spiritual poison in these people. He decided to write what he saw to the Missionary Bulletin that others would see what life was like on the coast and how much Christian medical work was needed.

Bella Bella

July 26th, 1904.

"Last week I went to see the Chinese foreman at one of the canneries. He had been having trouble with his Chinese workers and had taken an overdose of opium. The Chinamen, when they found him, carried him out into their small garden and beat him so vigorously over the arms, legs and chest with their slippers, previously moistened with water, that they made him black and blue. I was not called till next evening. He was still on his mattress in the garden. The Chinese expected him to die and so would not move him in China House fearing that his spirit would haunt the place afterwards. We wished to bring him to the hospital for treatment, but after parleying about half an hour his friends decided to keep him and treat him themselves. He died the next day. Apparently he had taken an overdose of the opium as an effective way of getting away from his troubles."[1]

Occurrences like this were not uncommon. To most Whites and Indians China House was somewhat sinister. It was a separate colony within the community and few outsiders penetrated beyond the docile exterior of these poor creatures, most of whom had been brought from Kwang-Tung province through "Barraccon Houses" whose agents went out into the villages rounding up emigrants with stories of instant wealth in the new land beyond the sea. Their migration to North America was an epic of suffering barely surpassed in inhumanity by the slave trade from Africa. Like animals they were herded onto overcrowded boats with the meanest of rations and almost total absence of sanitary facilities. Many died en route. Sometimes terrible riots broke out during the crossing.

When the *Ann Baynton* arrived at Portland, July 1881, for example, she bore the scars of a bloody battle that had raged among the three hundred and fifty Chinese aboard. Not far out from Hong Kong on the 15th of June trouble had erupted. One gang of coolies believed they were being deprived of rations while another group was being favoured. Armed with belaying pins, capstan bars and cordwood sticks they raged back and forth across the decks, splitting each other's skulls with the blunt

103

weapons. Pistol shots fired over their heads by the captain and crew failed to quell the riot. Finally, Captain Nason ordered the crew to throw pails of carbolic acid among the infuriated mob. This subdued them. But it was a wounded, weary ship and cargo that landed at Portland that summer of 1881.

By 1900 the head tax on Chinese immigrants was up to $100 from the $50 set in 1885. In 1902 a Royal Commission was established to look into the growing problem of Asian immigration. One result of this commission was that two years later the head tax was raised to $500. This tax, plus the fare for passage and a percentage "for the trouble" all had to be deducted from the Chinese workers' wages, which were already atrociously low. The result was that they received very little actual cash. Consequently, private enterprise being what it is, China House homebrew was a well known commodity around the cannery, the main market for the unpalatable product being the Indians. In spare time many of them roasted and packaged peanuts which they brought in by the sackful. But even these extras earned by ingenuity were often lost long before they boarded the steamer or returned to the city, for the Chinese were inveterate gamblers.

Many of the labour contractors were ruthless individuals devoid of human compassion. People like Charlie Suey, Yip Sang and his son Yip Him, while shrewd businessmen, were well established and highly respected. But other unscrupulous characters found in this labour market an opportunity for rapid gains. What wages were paid out could easily be won back by running a gambling den. Opium trade was brisk and profitable and many corners could be cut to save on expenses.

For example it was the contractor's responsibility to feed his crew of workers from the time they left the home port till their return at the close of the fishing season. The prescribed diet was rice, cabbage and fish. Chicken or pork was a treat enjoyed once a week at most. So it is not surprising that a Chinese contractor occasionally became the target of some irate worker's revenge.

Such was the case late one evening in the summer of 1921. Most of the passengers on the Union Steamship *Camosun* were asleep when an unknown Chinese came to the saloon asking for a pot of tea. "Paddy" Nicholls, the night steward was only too happy to oblige. He chuckled to himself thinking how the English and the Chinese were alike. Neither of them can get along without their tea, he mused. But a moment later he was scratching his head and looking at the spot where he knew his butcher knife had been. He decided to call Smith the Purser.

The two men were standing in a passageway talking about the missing knife and wondering what to do about it when the steady murmur of the engines was split by screams coming from one of the cabins. Quickly Nicholls and Smith ran to investigate. It was the cabin of Ma Toy, the Chinese contractor. Into the cabin crashed the Purser. He grabbed a blanket, threw it over the wild assailant, and in a moment had him disarmed.

But it was too late to help Ma Toy. He had been stabbed and gashed all over his body. When the *Camosun* landed at the paper-mill town of Ocean Falls the attacker was handed over to the police and Ma Toy was placed in the little company hospital, though everyone knew there was little hope for recovery.

China House was always a special worry to the cannery manager. It was not the occasional eruptions of violence that concerned him, for basically Chinese workers were docile and industrious. Though they were the target of much goading and teasing, they generally avoided contact with Whites, Indians and Japanese. But China House was regarded as a constant fire hazard.

The huge bunkhouse as originally designed was nothing more than two or three stories of long, loftlike dormitories, bare in the extreme. Once the crew moved in for the summer they scrounged packing boxes, scrap lumber and whatever material they could lay their hands on and proceeded to build individual cubicles around each bunk. Into this dark cloister the Oriental would crawl after his work was done. There he could lie, suck occasionally from his opium pipe and allow sweet oblivion to sweep away the misery of the day. No wonder the manager worried about fires.

105

A cannery manager was responsible for the success or failure of the season's work. Probably a graduate from the files of fishermen or workers, he was chosen for his ability to handle men and machines, for his knowledge of fishing and his ability with figures. In the early days the manager might be dumped on the beach with a pile of lumber and a few men. It would be his job to build the cannery, order supplies, negotiate through the Chinese and Indian bosses for labour, engage a fleet of fishermen and see that every aspect of the complex operation fitted together so that by the end of the season there was a pile of canned salmon to ship out and a set of books that balanced.

When Robert Draney along with the Victoria druggist Thomas Shotbolt decided to build a cannery, the old *Barbara Boscourtz* carried Draney and his supplies to the Inlet during a blinding snow-storm one late winter day. They had prospected and surveyed a site in what became known as Shotbolt Bay, but the snow made it difficult for the captain to tell exactly where they were. Eventually the *"Barbara B"* anchored and the supplies were floated ashore. Next morning Draney and his handful of men discovered that they were about three miles from the intended site. The steamer had weighed anchor and was gone, so there was nothing to do but to go ahead and build right where the cargo had been dumped on the snow-covered ground. That is how Rivers Inlet Cannery (better known as R.I.C.) came into being back in 1882.

Perhaps the best known and most beloved manager on Rivers Inlet was Frank Inrig. Those who knew him like to tell the story when he was at Standard Cannery on the Skeena River. He had started there about 1890 after coming from Scotland. In 1896 his fiancée came out to meet him and get married. Of course there was no minister at Standard Cannery. Frank was a Baptist. His bride-to-be was Presbyterian. So they compromised and went to Mr. Guard, the Anglican pastor at the Indian village of Metalakatla. Upon their return from the ceremony they stepped out of and steamer into a tiny dinghy. The current was running swiftly and as they stepped down the boat began to tip. In an instant they were tossed into the cold, muddy river wearing all their finery.

Frank Inrig was called the Dean of Managers on the Inlet. He built Goose Bay Cannery in 1927 and a few years later resigned as manager because of a mistake which he considered to be his fault although no one else accused him. From time to time the boiler had to be shut down and the tubes blown out. This was the engineer's job. It was not a complicated piece of work though once it was done the water to the tubes had to be turned on again before the furnace was started. On this occasion the engineer simply forgot to let the water into the tubes before firing up. When he noticed his mistake and opened the valve the cold water entering the hot pipes caused them to burst. Under normal circumstances a manager would have been within his right to fire the engineer for incompetence. Frank Inrig held to the view that the manager should be in control of every facet of the cannery's operation. He accepted the blame and resigned.

That was in 1930. Two years later Inrig started a plant of his own in Moses Inlet, an arm that branches off Rivers. But the industry was experiencing serious difficulties. He was unable to market his pack in 1935 and went bankrupt. That was the last cannery to be built on the Inlet. From then on there was a steady decline in the number of plants until Goose Bay, the last to cease operations, finally shut down in 1957.

When Frank Inrig resigned from Goose Bay the man who had been his bookkeeper and storekeeper took over managership. This was Francis Stone, son of Arthur the "peacekeeper". Francis was well equipped for the diversified duties of manager. Brought up in the old court-house beside Green's Cannery, he became acquainted with boats and engines earlier than most children learn to ride a bicycle. One of his greatest childhood adventures was to accompany "Pop" Stone on the police boat out to the mouth of the Inlet on a dark night, drifting without running lights and sneaking alongside fishing boats as they evacuated the Inlet at the end of the season. At that time the companies supplied gillnets on a rental basis and many of them were disappearing. Young Francis felt like a commander of the Queen's Navy whenever they nabbed a fisherman with a stolen net.

At that time the only connection with the outside world was the Union Steamship boat which made a trip to the Inlet every two weeks. The steamer's arrival was a social highlight at each cannery settlement. She would blow her hoarse warning, the sound reverberating between the mountains, then bear down on one cannery after another while the message spread like wildfire throughout the little communities.

"The boat! The boat! Boat's coming!"

Everything arrived by steamer. Supplies for the cannery, groceries for the store, grub for the cookhouse, clothing purchased by catalogue and news of what was happening "outside". But the steamer only came once every two weeks so news was often history before it arrived.

As a lad Francis Stone acquired a small radio receiver, a primitive piece of equipment which required sitting up half the night dickering with a dial before a broadcast could be picked up. He used to catch bulletins late at night. He would type several copies and drop these news-sheets at the canneries as he delivered lumber for Victoria Sawmill situated at the head of the Inlet. But it took quite some time before the old-timers began to appreciate his volunteer news service. When the steamer arrived they were always amazed to discover the reports Francis had left a week or two earlier were correct. At cannery after cannery someone would amble over to him and say, "You know what you said on that there little sheet when you was around — well, sir, the steamer was in and do you know it's a fact. Yes sir, it's a fact!"

It was incredible to them that Francis could hear voices in a little box, especially since it was usually silent through the day.

In later years every fisherman on the Inlet would lug a dry cell battery and radio onto his boat and listen religiously to Earl Kelly, the province's "Mr. Good Evening". For many years

Kelly was the fishermen's friend, bringing them news, weather and special personal messages.

Francis Stone always loved the smell of yellow cedar bow stems cut on the band-saw better than the harsh fumes of the cannery, but he possessed that ingenuity and versatility which was a prerequisite quality for a manager. When a little Indian girl died at Goose Bay Cannery, her people, according to custom, wanted to return with the body to their own village down near Powell River. But the steamer refused to take the body unless sealed in a metal-lined casket. Francis hopped onto his boat and went around the other canneries scrounging pieces of scrap metal. He even straightened out an old piece of stove pipe, soldered them all together and lined the casket to meet requirements. The job was done in the living room of the little house where the child's body lay while all the relatives looked on. Dr. Darby came down from Bella Bella to make out the death certificate. The casket was covered with a Union Jack and the whole group marched solemnly to the steamer.

Not all funerals were done with the same amount of dignity. When Dan McClusky found his brother Charlie dead in their trapping shack, he carried the body down from Moses Inlet on his back. It was in the winter of 1923-24, shortly after the Victoria saw-mill had burned, when Dan trudged in with his dead brother. A few Japanese fishermen were around the site, but they would not go near the body. Francis Stone was the only one who could be of any help. But Charlie McClusky could not be buried until an official death certificate was written, and the only person within miles empowered to do that was Arthur Stone, at the time away at Bella Coola. They decided to leave the body in the blacksmith's shop till Corporal Stone arrived. The days passed. Dan McClusky felt he could wait no longer and went back to his trap line. Meanwhile the body lay in the blacksmith shop, a region well skirted by the superstitious Japanese. At the end of ten days Francis decided that certificate or not, Old Charlie would have to be buried. He dug a hole in the bush, dragged the body into it and covered it as quickly as possible. Two days later his father arrived and accepted Francis' word that Charlie McClusky was really dead before burial.

Sometimes a cannery manager was faced with situations which called for cool nerves and a degree of courage more in keeping with the duties of a policeman than a businessman. George Johnston had been with B.C. Packers as engineer at their Dominion plant on the Skeena. In 1921 he came to Rivers Inlet to run the old Provincial Cannery in Schooner Pass. In 1928 he moved over to Beaver Cannery further up the pass toward the main inlet. There he was called upon to walk the most frightening few steps he ever expected to take.

It was on towards Fall and things had quieted down considerably. The main sockeye runs were past and many fishermen had vacated the Inlet. Around Beaver a few Smith's Inlet Indians and some Owikenos from up at the head of Rivers were fishing for dog-salmon, their families remaining in the terrace shacks reserved for them. It was week-end which meant there was no fishing. The government enforced prohibition of fishing, usually from Thursday at 6 p.m. till the same hour on Sunday evening, to allow "escapement" of salmon so that sufficient numbers would find their way to the spawning streams. For a great number of Indians it was an opportunity to indulge in the most popular diversion from work — drinking home-brew.

Home-brew was as common a commodity on the Inlet as the smell of fish. Forbidden by discriminatory laws to buy or consume liquor or beer in the normal way, the Indians were driven to the purchase of bootleg liquor at atrocious prices, or to the manufacture of this vile tasting home-made product. And when the Indians' pots ran dry the Chinese made a handsome profit selling their particular brand with results that were often disastrous.

So when George Johnston heard screams and a series of shots he had no difficulty guessing what was happening. Sure enough, a few Indians were "liquored" up. Two of them got into a fight and the loser, a young fellow from Smith's Inlet, grabbed a rifle from his boat, stationed himself unsteadily on the boardwalk at the end of the terrace, and was proceeding to pump bullets into the houses where women and children crouched in fear.

George started along the plank walk. The lad reloaded the rifle and raised it toward him. Still the manager kept walking, not fast, just a steady pace keeping his eye on the boy all the time. It seemed a long, long way to the end of the terrace. At any moment the young Indian might put him in his sights and pull the trigger. After all he had fired a number of rounds and there was no telling what was going on in his alcohol-soaked mind. George wondered if the fellow had gone completely mad, or if he was only trying to draw attention like so many of them. Perhaps he had made the wrong move venturing out along the narrow boardwalk like this. But there was no turning back now. He kept going.

Now he was within a dozen steps from the swaying rifle barrel. If the boy pulled the trigger there was no chance of missing. George stopped within arm's length. His thick Scottish accent had a rough kindness in it.

"You'd better give me that rifle and jump aboard your boat and have a sleep don't you think?"

For a moment the young Indian looked at him as though trying hard to focus. Then he seemed to recognize George. Everybody knew the manager.

"Why don't you just give me the rifle and go and have a good sleep. It'll make you feel better eh?"

This time he held out his hand as he spoke. The lad's face twitched. There was a moment of tense silence as the two men faced one another. Then the rifle was thrust forward.

"All right, George," said the Indian lad. He slumped forward and the manager caught him and helped him to the bunk of his boat. It was all a part of the manager's job.

Perhaps the wildness of the Inlet itself had much to do with the behaviour of those who lived there. The mountains soaring away from the water's edge, the afternoon breeze driving up the channel making green-grey water jump and dance, rain clouds

111

tumbling in from the ocean, all these features combined to make life on the Inlet an exhilarating experience. It was rough country far from the strictures of the city. Practically every move was made in combat with nature and in the end Nature sculptured those who lived there in her own image and likeness, a breed of rough-hewn individualists who loved freedom and the struggle of life on the coast.

During July the main run of sockeye arrives and excitement reaches its peak. Fish-fever drove the fleet in its wild search for the bonanza catch which every man hoped for but few managed to find.

Up at the Head boats pressed close to the boundary imposed by the Fisheries Department. On the falling tide they lined up and played out their nets between the white triangles that marked the boundary on either shore. Tempers wore thin in jockeying for position. Nets tangled together, propellers snagged, swearing in a dozen accents could be heard above the sputtering of motors and if the fishery guardian happened to be Ray La-Marsh a boat that drifted across the line was liable to be rammed. For Ray had his own theories about how to keep fishermen out of the prohibited area where fish were supposed to be free from the menace of nets.

Charlie Lord was Justice of the Peace in matters pertaining to Fisheries between the years 1932 and 1947. The old Indians liked and respected Charlie because he could speak Chinook and always explained the formidable legal language to them. He was a working man at heart and hated to impose fines on fishermen whom he knew needed every cent they could get. But he was also a Britisher with a strong sense of the dignity of law. Many fishermen were arraigned before him down by Dawson's Landing on a Saturday morning because their nets had drifted into restricted water.

From the boundary, past Round Mountain, into Moses Inlet, Brunswick Bay and by the old hospital now empty, gaunt and green with moss, the gillnetters drifted. They fished through Schooner Pass, so narrow that nets had to be woven across in a series of S's. Around Welch Island and in every nook and cranny of Darby Channel, out past ominous Swan Rock and onto Fitzhugh Sound the boats were strewn. They drifted off Long Point and slid down the Inlet with the falling tide. Sometimes a sleeping fisherman would awaken to discover his net had wrapped around the Haystack, a tiny island named for its shape. Further down an unwary gillnetter could get sucked into skookum-chuck at Draney Inlet when the tide flooded. Out past Goose Bay to Major Brown Rock when the Pacific swells pounded and washed at the bald stone outcroppings with eternal determination the boats reared and plunged in the waves, or bobbed lazily during a rare calm.

Once gasoline engines were introduced there were boats of all descriptions and sizes, ranging from "high-liners" rigged with the latest equipment and bristling with paint, to tired old tubs that barely stayed afloat. There were Japanese, Indians, Swedes, Czechoslovakians, Scots, Finns and Greeks. There were teenage boys working furiously, nervously. There were old salts whose rhythmic movements were not squandered on unnecessary labour. And for a few seasons two Vancouver girls were afloat on the Inlet. Their net seldom touched the water but each morning they would have a box full of fish to deliver, and it became general knowledge that the price of a nocturnal visit to their craft ran as high as twenty-five prime sockeyes.

In the days when the canneries were alive, even after the sockeye runs had passed and the main fleet had gone up to Milbanke Sound, Spiller Channel, Roscoe Inlet and Seaforth Channel for the Fall fishing, there were several hundred inhabitants who lived permanently amid the gathering mists and rains of the up-coast winter. About fifty Japanese families made their homes there. The Owikeno Indians settled back at their village on the river which drained the glacial waters of Owikeno Lake and its watershed. A number of Whites stayed around the cannery sites; some of them went trapping or hand-logging. Throughout the twenties in Draney Inlet, a large logging outfit nibbled at the dream of wealth which had lured them into that region of spectacular beauty — a dream they were never to realize. It added up to a sizable population throughout the winter.

But those days are gone forever. The canneries are closed now. Imperial, Vancouver, Victoria, Whonnock, McTavish, Strathcona, Provincial, Brunswick, Inrig, Shotbolt and Green's — today they are only silent blemishes on the shoreline. R.I.C., Kildala, Good Hope, Wadhams, Goose Bay and Beaver continue to be used as service depots and fish camps during the season, but when the boats leave a quietness settles over the place and the few old-timers who stay to hand-log, or trap, or simply to collect their pension cheques, are swallowed up in the mist and rain till the boats arrive next season.

Gone is the community spirit when on a slack Saturday the cannery tender loaded up with families and headed for some secluded beach to picnic. When the steamer's arrival was a social event, a chance to visit and catch up on news, when Dawson's Landing was the meeting place for trappers down from the bush to buy clean underwear and loggers in to pick up mail and grub for their camps.

There is something sad about the quietness of the Inlet today, once the fleet leaves.

CHAPTER **13**

Coastal Characters

The title grew from an innocent remark to the stature of a fully developed legend long before he died. It stuck to him like the engine grease and beaver gore that clung to his hairy arms and soiled combinations. Everyone who knew him had to agree that it was a title well deserved, for without a doubt Dan Mc-Clusky was "The Dirtiest Man on the Coast."

Dan and Charlie were not only brothers, they were great friends. Both men were renowned as crack shots with the rifle. Both were wiry and tough from years spent tramping along trails and hauling in hand-lines. For months on end they disappeared, living in the tiny shack they shared where their trap lines met. Charlie was the quieter of the two, but Dan was the dirtier. It was a hard blow for Dan when he found his brother slouched in a chair in the shack — dead.

"Still — a fella had to keep on a-goin in this here life," Dan had concluded, and so after a few days he left Charlie's burial in the hands of Francis Stone and headed back to the lonely shack and to his traps.

Dan McClusky was known to just about everybody who fished, trapped or logged north of Alert Bay. He was well liked as a rule, though few people ever accepted the hospitality of his little troller.

Wherever a few boats were tied up around a float it was usual to find a group of men crammed into the cabin of one of them spinning yarns about fish and fishermen, engines and boats, women and weather. The stories were told in an atmosphere thick with tobacco smoke, body odours, damp clothing, bilge fumes and fish scales. They were told in crescendos that were commensurate with the consumption of Hudson's Bay rum gulped from mugs. Even when tea or coffee was the going fare the subject material for discussion was the same, though it must be admitted that tea failed to produce the highlights of imagination that could be fostered when raconteurs were nourished from the rum jug or the home-brew pot.

Parties of this sort were a way of life on the coast. But not many of them were held on Dan's boat. It was cluttered with tools and toilet paper, pots containing the remainder of last Tuesday's stew and others containing hard paint brushes. Engine parts, an old 32 "special" rifle, magazines, ammunition, net-twine and assorted clothing littered the bunk. Spark-plugs, nuts, bolts and washers, pieces of wire and fish-lures shared the cupboard with grimy jars of jam. Just inside the door, acting as a step, was a bag of flour that was as black as the bilge. It must have been there for a year before he decided that the contents were beyond use. However, it was not the disorder of the cabin that repelled McClusky's visitors. Fish boats are inclined to be less orderly than those domestic areas fortunate enough to come under the surveillance of the feminine eye, and even if Dan's boat was an extreme example of a generally low standard, still this was not what kept visitors from accepting his hospitality. What bothered most fellows was that when one was handed a tin mug full of coffee there was no way of knowing whether or not it was the same receptacle Dan had used as a convenience through the previous night. Certainly McClusky's care in the matter could not be trusted.

Dan's dirtiness was proverbial. For a few weeks every year he stationed himself at Bella Bella in order to troll for cohoe on Milbanke Sound. When the trolling finished he invariably headed down to Beaver Cannery on Rivers Inlet to see Mrs.

116

Wilson. Mrs. Wilson was herself one of the characters of the coast. She was the daughter of a man by the name of Hunt who had been a Hudson's Bay factor at Fort Rupert. Her husband was for some years the bookkeeper at Beaver Cannery, but when he died she carried on as storekeeper and caretaker, living a total of twenty-five years in this cranny on the coast with its cluster of buildings, its interminable rain, swirling mists and creeping tides. She was something of a landmark. Well-known and beloved from one end of the coast to the other she bullied a company of crusty bachelors with a mixture of home-made pie and a firm tongue. Not the least of her accomplishments was her ability to force Dan McClusky to change into a new set of underwear and have a bath at least once a year.

Late in the Fall, after being exposed to Mrs. Wilson's grooming, Dan took off for the trap-line where he would lose all track of time. If he happened to arrive back on the Inlet in time for Christmas at Dawson's Landing it was a sheer stroke of luck.

Christmas at Jimmy and Jean Dawson's red-roofed float-house and store was a wonderful time of warm friendship and fun. If it had not been for the Dawsons or the Grahams over at Duncanby Landing, the Yuletide season would have been a cheerless time for bachelor fishermen and trappers, the winter watchmen at the canneries and old-timers like Joe and Agnes Moore who lived by themselves in a float-house drawn up in a sheltered cove. Jimmy and Jean, like so many who made their home up-coast, were Scots. Back in 1924 when he decided to start a general store of his own in the bay almost opposite Beaver Cannery, most of his friends thought he was crazy. But before long they were coming to him for all their needs.

Mops and pails, enamel pots and bright shining kettles, sieves and strainers, lunch pails and gum-boots, bear traps and flash-lights, ropes, rifles, frying-pans and bed chambers, clusters of eye-bolts, potato mashers, soup ladles and cable clamps, dangled from the ceiling of Jimmy Dawson's store. Heaps of rain gear, itchy-type underwear, woolen socks, coarse pants and flannel shirts tottered on shelves. Groceries, strong on the rolled oats, hardtack and beans, lined the wall behind the main counter. Most of the floor space was taken up with tall tiers of pails, bundles of brooms, sacks of rice and sugar, or coils of rope. Customers were confined to a hazardous pathway between great piles of stock.

Business was conducted in a manner appropriate to the informality of relationships on Rivers Inlet. Long before the advent of self-serve food markets, while Jimmy was limping back to the warehouse for some obscure item, customers at Dawson's Landing helped themselves, piled the goods onto the counter and waited for Jimmy to tally up the bill. There was often a considerable lapse between the time goods were received and the time they were paid for. But little Jimmy Dawson was good natured, soft-hearted, patient beyond imagination and a great believer in the basic honesty of his fellow men.

"I owe you a can of tobacco, Jimmy."

"I picked up a couple pair o' socks last time I was in Jimmy. How much do I owe you?"

"How much is them cans uv bullybeef, Jim?"

"Why, would you like to have a couple?"

"Hell no! I got a couple last time I was in. Figured I'd otta pay yu for them, that's all."

This is how business was done, not always but often enough, at Dawson's Landing and if Jimmy happened to be taking a little nip from the rum jug in the back room, well the bargains were terrific!

Scattered as they were along the fragmented coast, customers were as interested in the social benefits of shopping at Dawson's Landing as they were in procuring goods and groceries. It might take a couple of hours to buy a handful of copper nails. Jimmy Dawson did no advertising. He had no lures, no gimmicks. When a crowd gathered at his place on Christmas Day there was no suggestion of patronage. In a land of hostile climate, long wearying distances and much solitude, friendship could not afford to be phoney.

One Christmas Day George Johnston, who was winter watchman at Provincial that year, invited the gang over to his place for dinner. In the evening they were to repair to Dawson's Landing for more rum and the opening of presents. Dinner was over and cigars were going around when over the peals of laughter the putt-putt of an Easthope engine could be heard.

"Who on earth could be travelling on Christmas Day?" they all asked. George went to the door and looked out towards the floats. It was Dan McClusky. He watched him ease alongside, step onto the greasy planks and throw hitches through the rings. Not until he shut off the engine did Dan shout up towards the house. What he said took George completely by surprise.

"Hello there, George!" shouted Dan. "What the hell day is it? I sorta lost track."

For a moment George thought he was joking. Then he realized that Dan was coming back from trapping. He probably had not seen a soul for the past two months and certainly would not have bathed in that time.

"Well, I'll tell you," replied Johnston, "you're just in time Dan, it's Christmas Day. I've got a bunch of your friends up here and we're having a great old time. So come on, get up here, there's plenty of everything."

Dan joined the party, and manifesting his usual sense of priorities headed straight for the rum before wiping the most conspicuous layers of filth from his hands and arms. Most of what was removed was deposited on the towel. But that was about as close as one could expect to get Dan McClusky to wash without the aid of Mrs. Wilson.

McClusky eventually took ill and had to go to hospital. When George Johnston went to visit him he barely recognised Dan. He looked at the clean face, the arms and hands free of engine grease, not a fish-scale clinging to them, lying against the white sheets, and he could barely believe that this was the same Dan McClusky who would shave chunks off a beaver tail with a Jappanese plane and fry them in the iron pan that sat on the roof of his wheel house.

"You know Dan," said George, "this is the first time I have

119

ever seen you really clean." They all had a good laugh, Dan included. But it was one of his last moments of merriment. Not long after this he died of cancer.

Dan McClusky was one of the innumerable characters who, having rejected the complicated, burdensome life of city and town, found asylum in the wild freedom of the coast. They were as independent as men could be, living in contact with nature, existing by skill, ingenuity and perseverance against bitter physical odds. Far from the amenities of urban life, also far from the sham, the oppressive treadmill of moneymaking, of tax bearing and keeping up with imposed standards.

There was "Duffy", an ardent Communist in theory though much too independent to live in accordance with those theories. He was forever trying to pass "hot" fish (fish going bad) and he was an habitual creek robber. When Duffy set out for his trapline the only food he carried with him was a can of cornmeal. He would live off the land for months sleeping in lair-like shelters in the woods. He was found dead on the west coast of Queen Charlotte Islands and what little evidence there was suggested that he had poisoned himself accidentally by eating toxic clams.

"Peg-leg" (Charlie) Olsen was a pugnacious fisherman-trapper who thumped along the plank walks at up-coast canneries and who achieved infamy by shooting at George Johnston because George's collie had beaten his dog in a fight over a chunk of stolen venison. Olsen was a very thick-witted oaf of a man. He maimed himself pulling a shot-gun out of a skiff and a few years after the first accident he blew off several fingers in exactly the same way. He could neither read nor write and was so obtuse that in a discussion he would argue violently with those who were agreeing with him.

For years he hobbled around on a peg-leg whittled out of a piece of fir from the sawmill at R.I.C. Joe Moore had brought Agnes to the head of Rivers Inlet to visit some of her relatives, for Agnes was an Owikeno Indian. Of course, their visit was an opportunity to celebrate and the home-brew was flowing like water. Olsen was none too nimble at the best of times but with the effect of the brew he slipped, went crashing to the ground and snapped his wooden leg. Joe offered to make him a new leg with an air of beneficence that elicited from Olsen a stream of profanities which for sheer variety seemed to belie his dullwittedness. However, Joe went ahead with his project while Olsen sat on the ground hugging the home-brew jug. A four-inch boom auger was used to make the knee-cup, and since it was obvious to Joe that Olsen was hard on peg legs he decided to make a sturdier model, one which would not so easily splinter or crack. The only trouble was that it was so heavy Olsen could not lift it. After more whittling, several fittings and numerous swigs of brew, like a new-born moose Olsen finally clambered up onto his new leg, held in place by a mess of rope, twine and straps, and the occasion was celebrated with more swigs of brew.

Poor old Peg-leg probably never caught a mink in his life, but he saw the other boys heading out to their lines and felt that he ought to do the same. He would throw a tent, a few groceries and a gallon of rum into his round-bottom skiff and row into Schooner Pass where no one had ever caught a mink. There on the shore he would pitch his tent and camp until the rum was finished.

After shooting at George Johnston, Olsen was sent down to Vancouver to be tried for attempted murder. No one really liked to be around Charlie Olsen for long, because there was no telling when he might decide to use his crutch to redress some imagined insult or affront. Even helping him to his boat when the strap on his wooden leg broke was to risk an avalanche of profane abuse. Nevertheless, George had known him for a long time and he hated to see the old fellow in so much trouble. When an opportunity to reach Vancouver arose he decided to visit Olsen in jail, but upon arrival he was told, "Didn't you know? Mr. Olsen took a heart attack and died two weeks ago."

All the boys around Rivers Inlet, when they heard, agreed that it was just as well that way. None of them would have enjoyed testifying at the trial, not even the trial of cranky old Peg-leg Olsen.

Another tragic, if colourful, career was that of J. J. Stump. He was part Cherokee Indian, highly intelligent and, so long as it was beneficial to business, intensely religious. It was also common knowledge that Mr. Stump was bribing the Fisheries Officer with a bottle of rum at regular intervals to have him turn a blind eye to certain regulations not being fulfilled.

When the Kingcome Inlet cannery burned Stump was the recipient of much sympathy. But, when shortly after this tragedy the LeRoy Bay plant went up in flames suspicions were aroused. Especially since all of the buildings were razed without burning any of the wooden walks between. The man who actually set the fire disappeared. Stump served time for arson and upon his release from prison was last seen selling sandwiches and pickled eggs in Vancouver's skid row beer parlours.

One of the most beloved characters of the coast was not fisherman or canner, trapper, logger, storekeeper or manager but the man who for almost half a century tended the spiritual and physical needs of all these people regardless of race, occupation, religion or financial status. No figure was more familiar or more welcome than that of Dr. George E. Darby. Clad in glistening oilskins he could be seen rowing through the rain and landing on the rocks of a lonely lighthouse. Sleeves rolled up to the elbows he could be found peering down the throat of an Indian child on the boardwalk by the cannery shacks. He could be seen in wicked weather picking his way through the nest of rocks between Rivers Inlet and Smith Inlet going to the Village of Takush, or he might be found reading the Bible in Chinook at the humble home of an old Indian friend.

Darby took over the work at Bella Bella in 1914. Travelling in a variety of small boats the tireless doctor ranged the ragged shoreline from Smith Inlet and Egg Island to Kitamaat Village, pulling teeth, lancing boils, delivering babies, suturing wounds, setting limbs, doling out pills and medicines and performing more serious surgery back at the shingle-clad hospital.

For years he was obliged to meet emergencies, tragedies and epidemics with the most meagre facilities and supplies. His first operation was performed in the medical post built by Dr. Large under the light of a lantern held aloft by the school teacher, pressed into service due to the lack of nurses. Darby's ingenuity and inventiveness, and the adroit way in which he could adapt to the necessity of the moment were responsible for saving numerous lives. Once he took a piece of wire, shaped it into a probe and removed a quarter that had lodged in a child's throat. On another occasion, in a remote village, he scrubbed the kitchen table and used it as an operating table. In his early years as coastal doctor he contested with an Indian medicine man, and won. But towards the end of his life, at a splendid ceremony staged by the Bella Bella Indians, Chief Moody Humchitt bestowed upon him the name Wo-Ya-La "The Highest".

After forty-five years of quiet, persistent service, Dr. Darby died in Vancouver in 1962. But up-coast, fishermen of every racial background, trappers, loggers and pensioners lighthouse-keepers, officers and crew-men on the coastal steamers and the inhabitants of Indian Villages, all remember the durable doctor whose rugged kindness helped so many.[1]

Concern for one another was a way of life on the Pacific north-west. Those who lived up-coast and those who came north in search of fish, were often cut-throat competitors, uncouth in speech, fast fisted around the floats and as independent as the wind that worried the rigging of their vessels. But they would forego fish, spend hours going out of their way, even risk their lives, to help someone in distress. And this is still true.

John Moore, a short, broad-beamed man built close to the deck of his fish collector, and with a sixth sense about the sea and weather, is one of those coastal characters who, perhaps more than anyone else, has the knack of showing up when a "May Day" is called or just about the time when a man has given up hope. How many fishermen and mariners have been relieved to see the sturdy, green bow of the *Advise* splitting the waves no one may know for sure, but the regularity with which John saves ships and lives is positively uncanny.

John's father came from England and homesteaded in the

plains at the head of Kitimat Arm. Few were the amenities of that bitter valley in the days before Alcan built its smelter and nurtured the mushroom city that sprawls there now. One of the closest contacts with other people was at Kitamaat Indian village where the Methodist Church ran a girls' boarding school designed to make chaste, cooking, sewing, English-speaking Christians out of the native girls. Moore married the matron and took her off to his bleak homestead. This was John's mother. When she died the father repaired to the boarding school and once more managed to convince the incumbent matron on the advantages of matrimony.

With this background it is little wonder that John spent a number of years working for the United Church of Canada, running their mission vessel, the *Thomas Crosby IV*. Then in December 1955, he bought the *Advise,* a 45 ft. troller type vessel equipped with a 100 h.p. Cummings diesel engine that could push her along nicely at nine knots. He rigged her out for towing and for fish collecting and brought aboard his stepmother and a "mean cuss" of a "yeller" dog. John Moore soon had a reputation as one of the ablest seamen on the coast.

On a black, dirty night when few would have poked their bowstems past the end of the floats, John was "mugging-up" in the galley, listening with one ear to the crackling 2292 radio band. It was about two-thirty a.m. and blowing a wet southeaster, a bad night to be out. Suddenly the static on the radio cleared and a frantic voice broke through.

"I'm on the rocks! I'm on the rocks!"

As fast as it had blurted over the air the voice faded again and static closed in. John tried rousing other boats to see if they had picked up the signal. He called back to the boat in trouble asking for name and position. But for a long time there was no reply, so he started the engine and made ready to pull out. Suddenly the speaker barked to life again. It was Harry Unger.

Harry had gone off shore from Calvert Island about forty-five minutes running time. He had thrown out the net and climbed into his bunk, thinking that in spite of the wind he was far enough

124

from shore to catch a couple of hours sleep without running into danger. Within an hour the wind and tide had driven him right onto the breakers. Desperately he had tried to wind in the net, allowing what fish there were to wrap into the drum with the corks and web, but only about three-quarters of the twelve-hundred foot net was aboard when the boat was tossed over a small breaker. There was a sickening, grinding sound as the metal shoe from the keel to the rudder caught the rock. When he tried to steer Harry knew the rudder was damaged.

Out of the blackness around him greenish fangs of phosphorous light, the effect of millions of minute particles of sea life, seemed to gnash at the hull. The place was infested with rocks, and upon each of them the sea frothed in sinister fury. In desperation the fisherman threw over the anchor. It began to grab, but as he kicked forward for position the propeller whipped into the dangling net and the engines grunted to a stop. Now he was helpless.

When the *Advise* ploughed through the blackness around the end of Calvert Island and up the west shore, John picked out the running lights and mast lights of two gillnetters standing off the rocks, bewildered. They wanted to help, and were in touch with their unfortunate comrade by radio phone, but neither boat would venture among the treacherous rocks close enough to get a line to him.

It was about three-thirty a.m. when John nosed the *Advise* between the rocks. At precisely the right moment he hollered above the howling wind to his deck hand. The tow line sailed into the gloom. The *Advise* swung around and eased forward. Her broad stern shuddered and grumbled, and the water erupted into green light as the propeller whirled. The towline swished tight and the luckless gillnetter silently, obediently followed the *Advise* through the rocks, out into deep water, around to the sheltered side of Calvert and eventually across Fitzhugh Sound through Schooner Pass to Whadams where they tied the damaged craft alongside a scow. When it came time to pull the boat onto the grid for repairs they discovered, much to their amazement, that the anchor was lying in the mud below. They had dragged it all the way.

This is only one incident in the life of the square-jawed skipper of the *Advise*. In a sloppy south-easter he might be found guiding a foundering tug into the shelter of Smith Inlet, speeding with an auxiliary pump to a sinking seine boat, or towing a crippled gillnetter to harbour. Those who fish up-coast all agree that ''It's a funny thing the way John shows up at the right moment. Time and time again.'' He is another one of the characters who have made life on the coast what it is and who have grown in stature by the challenge of life on the coast.

Many of the old-timers are gone now. There was Charlie Kratz who used to pick up anything that was not nailed down. He wanted to build a shelter on the stern of his boat so that he could skin mink out of the rain, and when he could not find lumber for the project he tore an armful of one-by-two strapping from the back of some bunk houses at Beaver Cannery. On the way to his boat with the loot under his arm George Johnston stopped him and asked what he was doing. Charlie made his case so persuasively that George had to let him pass.

"After all," he said with genuine indignation, "It's not as though I took them off the front of the buildings. And them cracks that's left'll do no harm. Nobody lives in there except'n summer."

Harry Lynn was another familiar figure up-coast. For a few seasons Harry and Dan McClusky trapped together, but eventually Dan could take it no longer.

"All he ever does is sit on the damn bunk and twirl his beard. He never talks! what in the hell good is a partner who never talks?"

There was Lou Hogan and Charlie Hay, both of whom drowned when the *Louisa Todd* capsized. There was Fred Anderson — married to big Sally from Owikeno village. Old Fred ended ignobly in a drunken drowning after outwitting the water and the weather for sixty years. There were the two Petes, "Curley Pete" and "Black Pete". They were huge, powerful men,

126

one a Scot and the other a Swede, with twenty years difference in their ages, but a bond of friendship between them as constant as the sighing of the tides.

At the time of writing Pete McWilliams buys fish and sells gas at Christie Pass. In Vancouver, New Westminster and up the Fraser Valley, in skid-row hotels or white painted cottages with rose gardens, in rest homes and boarding houses lives a legion of men whose sinewy arms, now aching with age and arthritis, once mastered the oar and drew a living from the cold, grey water. Few, if any, are rich. Their names may never be recorded in the annals of serious Canadian history for they lived their lives hidden from view by the towering mountains, separated from the crowd by the surging seas. Many of them were as wild as the waves that clawed the wrinkled beaches, yet with barely an exception they were loyal to the code of the sea. They could fight desperately on a Saturday and drown for one another on Sunday night. Their days were fitted with few comforts. A mug of hot coffee gulped in the morning drizzle, a swallow of rum, a hot bath in the sulphur spring at Kimsquit Arm. Yet few would have traded for a tamer life, for once fishing gets into a man's blood and the salt air saturates his soul there is no escape. And the chances are he will become a coastal character.

CHAPTER **14**

Port Essington and the King of Skeena

Skeena! Broad mouthed, beautiful Skeena! Three hundred and fifty miles of breathtaking splendour, with a drainage area of over fifteen thousand square miles, the "River of Mist" or the "Water of the Clouds" is alluring in her charm, though truculent in disposition. For sixty years along her lower banks and around her mud-stained mouth the salmon industry raged with a fury that was in keeping with her own turbulent, untamed career. And the man whose will dominated the scene for half of that period was big Robert Cunningham.

When Robert Cunningham left his home in Tullyvally, Ireland, and set sail for the North-west Coast, it was with an ardent desire to work for the Kingdom of God among the heathen natives of the region. With his tall, athletic frame and massive strength, his penetrating blue eyes and sharp, lilting voice he ought to have been a valuable asset to the missionary spearhead being conducted under the zealous leadership of the famed "Father" Duncan. But his association with the Church Missionary Society was to be a short-lived one for Robert Cunningham soon found greater satisfaction and success in hewing out an earthly kingdom for himself.

Cunningham joined the mission toward the end of 1862, the year in which Duncan and fifty native men, women and children climbed into their canoes and paddled twenty miles south of Port

Simpson to Venn Passage, where they formed the "Christian" village of Metlakatla. Whether it was the austere quality of Duncan's Christianity replete as it was with lashings for offenders of the fifteen point Mosaiclike law that caused the rift, or the fact that Robert married Elizabeth Ryan, one of the parishioners, may never be known. Cunningham was in all probability too human a man to live under the stern theocracy at Metlakatla. In any case he left the Missionary Society's service in 1864 and went to work for the Hudson's Bay Company. A few years later he and Thomas Hankin built a store at Woodcock's Landing (Skeenamouth or Skeena Bay) on the north shore of the Skeena River, but when they ran into difficulties with Woodcock over the land survey the partners decided to look for a new location. In 1871 Cunningham took out a pre-emption at a spot on the south bank called Spokeshute, where the Tsimshians used to congregate in the Fall after their summer fishing activities. (Spokeshute means Fall camping ground). Here the big Irishman built his trading post and named it Port Essington, the name given to the whole river mouth by Captain George Vancouver.

At first Port Essington had little to commend it as a port of call for the Hudson's Bay Company steamer *Otter* which was the only commercial freighter on the coast at the time. Cunningham was determined to have the benefit of the steamer so when she hove in sight one late evening he had some of his Indian friends light dozens of fires along the beach and hang coloured blankets on bushes and trees behind the flames in order to give the impression that the settlement was worthy of a stop.

Before long such deception was not necessary. Gold in the Omineca country lured men along the Skeena Valley into the interior. The Skeena itself was scoured for the precious metal and on Lorne Creek, Cunningham and others operated claims that produced well. All this meant a population influx and Port Essington became the popular starting point from which prospectors and miners made the arduous trip upriver.

Freighting was done initially by canoe. Manned by five sturdy Indians these huge cottonwood dugouts could carry a load of two tons each which under favourable conditions would be landed at Hazelton 160 miles upstream in about fourteen days The return journey took only two days. In 1890 the Hudson's Bay Company built the *Caledonia* and the following year this one hundred foot stern-wheel river-steamer, under the command of Captain Oden, made the first successful journey to Hazelton, and a new era of transportation came to the north country.

Even after the *Caledonia* was cut in two and lengthened by thirty feet, even after she was towed to Victoria and her engines were placed in a new and better *Caledonia,* Cunningham continued to employ Indian dugouts powered by paddles. But by 1900 the competition was being felt, or perhaps by that time he was convinced that stern-wheelers were profitable. In any case he decided to put his own river boat, the *Monte Christo,* into the run.

Hudson's Bay Company responded to Cunningham's entry by building the *Strathcona.* A year later Cunningham replaced the *Monte Christo* with the *Hazelton,* skippered by Captain Bonser. Almost immediately Hudson's Bay Company countered by putting the *Mount Royal* into operation with Captain Johnson at the helm and thus commenced one of the most colourful rivalries in the history of Canada's North-West.

The journey was a battle against the river all the way, a strenuous ordeal for the boilers of the river-boats, a taxing challenge to the wits and endurance of the skippers. Why Bonser and Johnson added to their dangers and difficulties by turning the trip into a perpetual race for the fastest round trip can only be understood by those who know the dauntless half-tamed spirit of the men who lived in that country before the comforts of road, railway and air travel.

The flat bottomed steamers followed the course of the sockeye. Smoke roaring from their tall stacks, the vessels clattered through Little Canyon. Past the silent mountains, the gaping mouths of tributaries that bled from the hearts of distant hills, past statuesque mountain goats disdainfully watching from their lofty ledges, the straining steamers worried their way through the cold, grey water. Eighty miles from the sea they winched themselves through the tough current of Kitselas Canyon by attaching a cable to the shore. They stopped now and then to take on cordwood, and if at all possible made sure that none was left for whoever was behind. They fussed and snorted past drab Indian villages like Minskinish, called the "Holy City" because the missionary there would not permit tobacco smoking nor steamer landings on Sundays; Kitwanga with its tall totems; Andemaul and Kitseguecla. They groaned over "Hardscrabble Rapids", past "Devil's Elbow", the "Whirlygig", "Klootchman's Canyon", "Beaver Dam", where only one safe passage between the submerged boulders existed, then on through the boiling water of "Hornet's Nest". And above all the clatter reverberating from the canyon walls, the aching engines and the rage of the river, above it all could be heard the thunderous oaths of Johnson and Bonser as they urged on their ships and wished upon another a rapid journey to the place where the boiler furnaces never go out.

The competition finally ended one day with Cunningham's *Hazelton* being the somewhat disputed champion after a dramatic neck to neck fight in which Johnson tried to run the *Hazelton* into shallow water. Bonser turned his ship hard to starboard just at the right moment, catching the *Mount Royal* amidships and pushing her against the opposite bank where he left her crippled and proceeded upstream amid the whiz of rifle shots fired by the irate Johnson. This ended the racing. Indeed, the *Mount Royal* ended her career tragically a few years later when she struck "Ring-bolt" Island. All the passengers were landed safely on the Island, but finally the captain could hold her no longer. The current suddenly flipped her over and six crew members were drowned.

The *Mount Royal* was carrying down thirty thousand dollars in gold dust when she was swept to destruction. But, gold was no longer the great attraction as the rush of miners and prospectors was well past by this time. Port Essington was still the terminus for the more settled upriver traffic but her twelve foot plank walk called Dufferin Street resounded to the clomp of

131

boots brought by another enticement, the wealth of the river. Salmon!

Robert Cunningham had encouraged the Indians to settle by setting aside a large portion of land for them. He sold other lots to settlers and entrepreneurs of varying degrees. By 1876 when the North West Commercial Company built the first salmon cannery on the Skeena at Woodcock's Landing, a bustling community was already in existence across the river at Port Essington and it was inevitable that the fishing industry would drive its pilings into the beaches of this new town where Cunningham was king.

The days of the gold rush were rowdy but no more so than the wild, ribald days of canning on the Skeena. Soon three canneries sprawled out over the tide flats at Port Essington, one of them belonging to Cunningham, naturally, and by 1906 the mouth of the river was blighted with fourteen of these seething shed-towns, each spewing smoke and steam into the air, each excreting tons of offal, garbage and sewage into the water.

Next to the Fraser, Skeena is British Columbia's largest river both in size and in salmon production. Between 1900 and 1938 the catch of sockeye in northern waters (including the Nass) exceeded the catch in the Fraser area for thirty-two out of thirty-eight years. About twenty per cent of the total sockeye salmon catch of British Columbia comes from the Skeena. No wonder the canners and fishermen flouted the cheerless climate of the north. Indians from upriver, Japanese from Steveston, white fishermen from Vancouver and New Westminster, as many as thirteen hundred of them, clogged the river with their gillnets.

The Skeena is full of snags and shoals so it was not uncommon to see an unwary fisherman high and dry on a bar with his net stretched across the sand, fish flopping, seagulls pecking out the eyes, eagles swooping to carry them off, and other fishermen drifting past, laughing and tossing jibes.

"Hey there Johnny! Youse a dry land fisherman — eh?"

"Howsa sand-hog?"

"How comes you don' wanna get you net wet?"

132

Close by Kennedy Island which stands in the mouth of the river, the incoming tide meets the outgoing current in such a way that at a certain stage a violent circular movement is set up. This was the "Glory-hole". Fish coming in with the tide would sometimes be trapped in this whirlpool till the water rose high enough to enable them to swim over an adjacent sand bar. It was a risky business to go into the Glory-hole but the men would drag their skiffs up onto the bar and play football while waiting for the tide, for there was always a chance of striking a thick school and pulling in a full net.

Over at Claxton cannery Isaac Benson took his job very seriously. Tom Wallace would give him the cue. Then Isaac would pull his limp fedora a little firmer onto his head and strut around the cannery officiously bleating on a battered bugle and interspersing the unmelodious notes with lusty hollers.

"All the mans ready fo ta Glooooy-hole! All the mans ready fo ta Gloooooooy-hole!" he would shout, whereupon a mad scramble of skiffs would scurry to the swirling water and drop their nets. As many as thirty boats might be caught in the conglomeration. Their masts were like a gaunt forest of limbless pines. Hulls crunched together. Nets become hopelessly entangled. Oars clashed and snapped — sometimes over the skulls of neighbouring boat pullers. The whole mess was kept in motion by the tide and from the vortex of this mad confusion there arose a tumult of profanity mingled with the exultant "ya-hoos" of those who were lucky enough to hit fish. Damage to gear and equipment, not to mention the fishermen themselves, often ran high in the Glory hole, but many were willing to take the chance because sometimes there would be a school of fish behind the bar, and a net full of Skeena River sockeye hanging by their gills was just about the most beautiful sight a fellow could hope to see.

At high-water slack the broad mouth of Skeena could lie like a placid lake, a sanctuarylike stillness capturing the mountain-framed scene. Then without warning the mood of the river would change. The sharp chop of wind whipped waves would slap the

133

planking of the fishing skiffs. Spray splattered the glistening oil-skins of the men. Rain, endless rain, stabbing with penetrating cold, chased the jocund spirit of the fleet so that for each man it became a lonely vigil of misery and endurance.

For the weathered fishermen it was a hard enough life, but when greenhorns managed to acquire gear and a license, the results were often disastrous. The fate of two who rented net and boat to fish the Skeena in 1906 could be the story of scores who learned too late the treachery of the tides. A sudden wind sprang up. Many of the fleet were blown out to deep water where they fought with the waves till the cannery tug came along to pick them up and bring them to safety. The two inexperienced lads were unable to keep the bow into the waves. When the tug found their skiff it was a dismal sight bobbing on the cold water bottom up. The crew of the tug latched onto the capsized boat in order to tow it to the cannery. They noticed a heavily weighted line running from it and began to haul it in. To their horror up came one of the fishermen. Somehow the end of the rope had wrapped around his wrist. His partner was never found.

Men who work hard and flirt with danger to earn their bread invariably play hard when their toil is over, and frequently the harsher the physical environment the wilder the recreation. At Balmoral, Haysport, Port Edward, Claxton, Inverness or any of the cannery settlements around Skeena the week-end was characterized by a majority of the inhabitants being thoroughly intoxicated for as long as the supply of booze and their individual constitutions held out. But for sheer debauchery, unabashed carousing, glorious mêlées and occasional gory murders, nothing could match Port Essington.

Well into Saturday night the planks of Dufferin Street were splashed with yellow light falling from the windows and doors of shops and restaurants. A seething melange of men kept the thoroughfare in perpetual motion, wading from the shadows into pools of light and back into the shadows. They leaned against the clapboard wall of Cunningham's store like limp anemones left hanging when the tide recedes. They staggered in and out of the Caledonia and the Queen's hotels. They weaved past Morrow and Frizzel's meat market, past the Anglican Church into Kamada's store and restaurant, or back again to Hepenstall's pool room and Lee Wing's eating place. The one thing not available at any of the main street stores could be purchased in certain shacks situated beyond the A.B.C. Packing Company's Boston cannery, and a regular cortège of customers beat a path to and from the hospitable quarters of Blanche Heart and her cohorts.

One evening three drunken fishermen crashed into Kamada's place and began smashing things. No one paid particular attention. They were simply on the rampage for some fun, a common sight about town. Roaring with laughter they drove the proprietor and his helpers from the store with a blitz of crockery. It was a very foolish thing to do.

There was no change in the expression of the hardworking little Japanese Canadian, at least none that could be detected, as he made his way with solid step to the house of a friend. Yet deep down in his soul a flame sprang to life, a flickering candle enclosed since the days of his ancestors in a mantle of quiet industry and apparent insouciance. When he returned to his shop he was no longer Kamada the storekeeper, the restaurateur serving soup, he was Kamada the samurai.

Moments after he and his pack of friends entered the shop one of the fishermen came crashing out, eyes bulging in terror, hands clutching at his throat in a vain effort to stop the blood that spurted between his fingers and splashed for a hundred yards along the boardwalk. He fell, head lying at an awkward angle to reveal a gaping throat wound stretching from ear to ear. Another fisherman was carried out later on a stretcher. He spent months in hospital, paralyzed as a result of a knife stab in the spine. Befitting the lenient law of the north the Japanese were given jail sentences for carrying things too far.

Port Essington was not a town. It was an organism. It throbbed with life, it retched and ached with suffering. In summer it was a place of clanging machinery, cluttered wharfs, stinking cannery waste, leaking steam, alcoholic weekends, furious fishing and roaring brawls. It was a conglomeration of clapboard and corrugated metal, cedar pilings steeped in the river or standing in muskeg, salmonberry and salal bushes clawing at plank walks and sloughs that trickled to the beach like running sores. And there were the milling crowds of people, Indians, Chinese, Japanese, Greeks, Swedes, Irishmen, Scots, Finns, Hawaiians, Norwegians, Czechs, Germans and Englishmen. The highways of the world crossed on that little rocky point jutting out into the Skeena. The people were there because of the living wealth of the river and when fishing ended for the week and the belts in the canneries stopped whining, they shuffled and shoved from one end of the community to the other looking for diversions.

A regular attraction in direct opposition to the basic joys offered by Blanche and her girls was the band of the Church army, composed mainly of Indians. Early in the season they presented a formidable array of "strength in the Lord". In front of Herman's cannery (later Wadham's) the band would congregate to blast forth the blessed battle-cry of righteousness. But as the season wore on the strength of the band dwindled, for it was an axiom of Church Army dogma that no alcohol fumes were ever to be blown through the sacred mouthpieces of its instruments. Consequently by the end of the summer, a pathetic trio piped the persistent call of salvation to the unheeding passers-by. It would be well into the winter before the backsliders were all re-converted, re-redeemed and reinstated.

Winter was when the few permanent residents breathed a sigh of relief and took up their routine of social events. With the hectic days of the fishing season past married women ventured to take a walk up to the dam or along the crumbling path to the old sawmill. Church socials were held in winter and if someone died there was time to make it a worthwhile event. The sprawling canneries slumbered through the dismal winter. China House was shuttered. Dufferin Street was strangely silent. Winter was in fact an annual premonition of the final silence that was to fall upon Port Essington.

In a way, the axe was first laid to the roots of the community with the death of its founder, Robert Cunningham. The big Irishman's life was a colourful tapestry of triumph and tragedy. In a few years he built a fantastic commercial empire in the north, an empire that included mining and lumbering, salmon canning and fish-oil refining, a cold storage plant and a fleet of tugs, river-boats, construction, real estate, hotels, fur trading, the operation of the town hall and general merchandising. Wherever there was money to be made, Cunningham would be there making it.

Others have become wealthy by wresting riches from the north country. They invariably move out, build comfortably in the fashionable quarters of Vancouver or Victoria, and continue to drain off benefits from their enterprises. Robert Cunningham, however, lived in the north and loved it. His satisfaction came not from the money he acquired, but from the process of acquiring it, a sort of sheer carnal pleasure from pitting himself against the untamed wilderness, and though he amassed a fortune he acquired no airs.

He was very fond of a game of cribbage, a pastime not held in high repute by some of the more enthusiastic members of the Church. One Sunday he and a few friends were enjoying a game when the Church bell rang. Cunningham scooped up the cards and thrust them into his pocket. "Come along gentlemen," he said, "it's time for Church. Guess we can finish our game later."

There was no minister at Port Essington at the time and the task of preaching naturally fell to the erstwhile missionary who was just as energetic in oratory as he was in industry. Part way through the sermon he pulled out his handkerchief to mop his brow and to the horror of the worshippers fifty-two cards fluttered around the pulpit and scattered along the floor.

Robert Cunningham was a friend of the Indians. They trusted him, which is saying a lot, for hitherto they had been given little reason to trust any of the white traders. Natives from upriver would throw a pile of furs onto the floor of his trading post and ask, "How much they worth Mr. Cunningham?"

When they were assessed the Tyee white man would state the value.

"You've got two hundred dollars worth there Benjamin. What would you like money or goods?"

"You pay me later maybe in the Fall after I back from fishing —O.K.?" It would be O.K. He knew Mr. Cunningham always paid up.

The availability of actual cash was a problem in early days, for there were no banks. Cunningham overcame this obstacle by having coinage of his own manufactured in the form of brass discs stamped with his name and various values. Even these trading tokens were in short supply from time to time and Cunningham sometimes found himself without the means to pay a client for furs or services. Tearing off a chunk of tough wrapping paper he would scribble out an I.O.U. for the amount. Some of these notes returned to him months, even years later, having passed through many hands. They may have been soaked in the Skeena and dried before a camp fire, crumpled in a pocket or stored in a tea pot for several seasons. They came back tattered and torn, limp and begrimed, often barely legible, but they were always honoured.

When Collin's Telegraph Line was under construction local Indians were hired to clear the right-of-way. They were paid in new Canadian dollar bills, very suspicious looking pieces of paper which the natives hurried to exchange for Robert Cunningham's trading tokens, which they knew they could trust.

The north-west coast had wealth for those whose spirits were stout enough to stand the rigours of her chilling breath and rugged ways, but she also exacted her price. Peter Herman, who was Cunningham's prime rival in Port Essington, was towing logs in a skiff. The logs snagged, a loop of cable caught Herman's ankle, he was whipped out of the skiff and drowned at the age of forty-four.

Jimmy Adams was a well-known and much respected community figure at Port Essington. He was a little Scotsman with not much formal training but with a basic sense of honour and honesty that won for him the position of Justice of the Peace until a magistrate was appointed. Jimmy claimed to be responsible for saving Port Essington from the great flu epidemic that followed World War I. He ran the ferry service across river to Haysport and other points, and during the epidemic he consistently refused to bring passengers to Port Essington if he thought there was the slightest possibility of their being infected or having contact with the disease. There may have been some truth in his claim too, for though the coast was severely hit with the terrible scourge not one case of flu was reported in Port Essington. One day Jimmy Adams brought a telegram from Haysport over to Claxton Cannery right at the mouth of the river. It was rough and the boat took a battering but he made it safely and snuggled the boat alongside the wharf. The tide was low so he climbed onto the deck beside the wheelhouse in order to hand the telegram to one of the men above. The boat lurched and Jimmy was crushed like a fly between pilot-house and wharf.

Robert Cunningham also knew the inexorable demands of the ruthless river and the undulating tides. He and Elizabeth had five children. Three of them died in infancy. What use is there speculating, wondering if urban medical care could have saved them? They died. Two strong boys survived and what a pride and joy they were to their Indian mother and their big, sentimental, Irish father. Then the sea took John, the eldest, when he was seventeen. In 1888 Elizabeth Cunningham volunteered to go with the Reverend Mr. Shelton and his wife to visit a sick man downriver. Their canoe split and they were all drowned.

Five years later Robert Cunningham married Florence Bicknell. They had three children, but Robert never set eyes on his youngest. He died in April 1905, and Edith was born several months after his death.

The story goes that at the funeral of Robert Cunningham hundreds of natives congregated from all over the coast, from the Nass, the Skeena, Port Simpson and Kitamaat, for he had been their trusted friend. Haidas crossed over from the Queen

Charlottes. They came from as far as Bella Bella, Bella Coola and Alert Bay, even from Nootka on the west coast of Vancouver Island and from Mission City up the Fraser. Dignitaries of the Church were present as well as representatives of the canneries and other industries.

At one point in the proceedings there seemed to be a slight stir. It happened so quickly and with such ease that few realized what was taking place. The Indians simply closed in around the coffin, bore it away to a waiting canoe and pushed out to sea, a virtual armada of canoes containing some two thousand natives chanting solemn dirges and mournfully beating their drums. They would bury the "King of Skeena" among their chiefs. To this day only a few Indians know where Robert Cunningham rests, so the story goes.

With the building of the railway on the opposite bank a lot of trade bypassed Port Essington and a sickness settled into the timbers of the town. Fire snatched a building occasionally and unlike the old days when new structures would spring up overnight, the charred remains stood gaunt and ugly until the undergrowth pulled her modest blanket of green over the scar. By 1936 the Dominion Fisheries Department moved the fishing boundary to a point ten miles downstream from the original line. Canneries at Haysport and Port Essington were left inside restricted waters. The fleet moved out. Faster boats made transport of fish to fewer canneries possible and Port Essington died. For a while a few Finnish families and some Indians lived in scattered shacks on the site, but decay carried on her silent, sinister work and desolation staked her claim among the ruins that lined Dufferin Street. Then in 1961 fire consumed what was left of Port Essington, and now the wilderness is silently, inexorably reclaiming her own.

CHAPTER **15**

The Case of Bill Cook
and His People

Cold drizzle seemed to hang in the morning air as the *Winnifred C* pranced over the waves of Johnstone Strait in search of fish. She looked like some marauding sea-wolf mercilessly tracking down her prey. Before her bow a pile of whitening water split and fell away in waves that raced towards the green shores. Heaped on board her stern was the seine net, 300 fathoms of tough nylon mesh with its orange sponge corks piled to the starboard and twenty-one hundred and sixty pounds of lead line lying opposite, ready to play out over the table roller. On top of the net sat the skiff with a line running back to the winch.

Bill Cook, the skipper-owner was at the wheel behind the dodger. Webs of water wafted into his bronze face and ran in little rivulets down behind the collar of his oilskins. It was the seventeenth of August, 1960, yet it was bitterly cold. The seven man crew of the *Winnifred C* would never forget the date.'' Bill Cook peered into the gossamer rain scanning the sea for jumpers.

About eleven thirty on that fateful morning he swung around the point into Good-hope Bay. That was not the proper name for the place, but Bill's people, the Nimpkish Band of Alert Bay, had called it that for as long as he could remember. He buzzed down to the crew and they tumbled on deck pulling on rain gear as they came.

What a difference from the old days when seining was done

141

by staking one end of a six-hundred foot net to the shore near a stream, sweeping around the fish and drawing them onto the beach. In those days only the Indian was allowed to seine and each band had its own location. Bill could not remember fishing like that, for he was only in his thirties now, but his father-in-law, Jim Sewed, who was a virtual encyclopedia of information about the early days, had told him. As a boy Jim had started out drag-seining at the mouth of the Nimpkish River, then he had moved to skiff-seining. A large crew working out of two skiffs would encircle a school of fish and laboriously draw the purse line by hand. It was tough work in those days.

Even after Captain Dan MacDonald introduced the use of steamer and scow it was still heavy work because the net had to be hauled by hand. MacDonald had been a mountain of a man who used to bath in a bluestone tank. Around 1918 he had been regarded as a paragon of modernity. With a scow and the old steam-tug *Kildala* he reaped in tons of pink salmon off Jenny Bay, Frenchman's Creek or up at Humpback Bay. It was Dan MacDonald who had introduced the use of steam-tarred seines and who invented the idea of salting the net down to preserve it over the winter. Seining had come a long way since then.

Bill slowed the engine gradually till it was idling. He threw the clutch out of gear and allowed the *Winnifred C* to slide across the bay. All the time his eyes kept roving back and forth looking for the sign that would tell him where to make a set.

With the power block he could make ten or more sets a day, even allowing for some running time. Although the power block and winch had revolutionized seining, eliminating much of the arm-rending labour, the number of fish had diminished and the boats had increased. Gone were the days when a seine crew could fill a waiting scow with tons of salmon. Now the fish had to be hunted down. A good seining spot might have a dozen boats each waiting their turn to make a set, and when that turn came the catch might be only fifty fish, or twenty-five, or none. The catch had to go eleven ways: two-and-a-half shares to the boat, one-and-a-half to the net and the remaining seven shares were split among the crew regardless of the number of men. There would be a bonus, part of the boat and net share, for the skipper.

With over four-hundred seiners scouring the coast, not to mention the gillnet fleet of over 4,500 and perhaps 3,000 trollers, it was little wonder that fish were scarce. Two years earlier the average net earnings of seine skippers had been $7,412 but that was a "bonanza" year, a sheer freak of good luck which could not be expected often, and Bill knew it. In 1957 the average had only come to $3,467.

Bill saw the jumper. Immediately he threw the clutch into gear and speeded for the spot. The skiff man and his helper were ready, crouched in the boat which had been lowered behind the stern and which now trailed along on top of the wake.

"Let 'er go!" yelled the skipper. The boat shot out from behind the *Winnifred C* and the oarsman pulled hard against the drag while the net tumbled off the table leaving an orange tracer of corks in the wake. Out in a wide sweeping arc went the seiner till a gaping crescent of net lay facing into the tide. Then the towing began. The skiff-man pulled on the oars. The plungers tossed the lead, hauled it in and tossed again, and again, scaring the fish if there were any lest they sneak around the end of the net and escape. The *Winnifred C* churned at the water. The cork line tightened and the bite began to close. Twenty minutes was the legal time for towing and most skippers kept the bite open for as long as possible in the hope that more fish would be trapped in the circle of net. The whole set would take about an hour, providing nothing went wrong.

Bill was proud of his men. They worked together like a team. When the bite was closed the skiff-men gathered up the slack corks and piled them in layers over the end of their boat. Two of the crew hauled on the corkline at the stern of the seiner to keep the net from bunching up around the rudder. The plungers were working steadily, methodically. Bill went to the winch and began drawing in the purse line while one of the lads laid it out neatly to one side. The purse line ran through brass rings at the bottom of the seine. As it was wound in the net closed like a

purse and the fish were trapped. The rings were just coming to
the surface when the accident occurred.

Bill reached around to catch the brake lever so that he could
shut off the winch quickly once the rings were out of the water.
As he did his arm caught and in a flash he was pulled off his feet.
He was thrown over the purse line and drawn in with the rope
till his face came hard against the moving wheel. It all happened so quickly that no one had a chance to help him. He had
the sensation that the ship and the whole world were being
thrown on top of him, but somewhere in the conglomeration of
flying mountains and mast, sky and pilothouse, guy-lines and
deck, he caught a fleeting glimpse of the winch lever. Miraculously, he managed to trip it.

Years later he would remember lying there on the wet deck
with the drizzle hitting his face, thinking . . . thinking that he
could not move his legs. From that moment Bill never walked
again.

One of the boys radio-phoned for a seaplane, but when it
arrived and Bill was strapped onto a stretcher they found it
impossible to get him from the seiner into the plane. Just then
Reg, his father, who had heard the message over 2318 and had
speeded to the spot, came alongside with the *Cape Lazo*. He
took Bill to Alert Bay. From there he was flown to Vancouver.
Two years later Bill Cook returned to Alert Bay, permanently
paralyzed from the chest down. But he returned to fish.

The doctors had advised him to learn some other useful occupation. In an industry that is gruelling enough for the fit it
seemed senseless to expect that Bill would ever fish again. But
he wanted to prove that he could still handle the *Winnifred C*,
and after drawing his own idea of what could be done the doctors consented and the seiner underwent renovations for her
skipper. Inside the wheelhouse a chair lift was installed that
ran to the bridge, while on the bridge itself, another chair was
set on rails so that it could move from side to side. The dodger
was replaced with plexiglass. Two years after the accident the
Winnifred C was under command of her owner again, and Bill's

wife, Dora, with the grace of a queen and the loyalty of a legendary princess, went to sea with him, steering the vessel, acting as his legs.

This story is told because it refutes the lie that is so often accepted about the coastal Indians. They are regarded as lazy and shiftless, unreliable and lacking in perseverance. Some of them are. And so are some white people. But among the finest fishermen on the coast today are many native Indians, and the heroism and courage of Bill Cook is evidence that we have not yet robbed them of all their self-esteem nor plundered completely the treasures of their heritage. In the desolation which we bestowed upon them, here and there the ancient spirit of a proud people still lives on.

Once the Indians of the coast knew no want. Their camps and villages were planted on the fertile waterways that brought food to their feasting bowls. Then came the white man buying fish for blankets and beads, plundering the runs and teaching the natives to do the same, destroying wherever he went. When it was almost too late we decided that regulations ought to be imposed to conserve the salmon. The Indian was to be allowed his ancestral rights to fish for food. But gradually, insidiously, the spectre of White law encroached upon these rights. Permits had to be secured to fish for food. At first it was a mere routine. Then the permits, which were issued at the discretion of the local fisheries officer, became subject to various limitations, and the native who had fished a family stream for generations now had to ask permission before he could hunt for food. He might be limited to a few days fishing. He might even be denied a permit.

In a sense all of this was necessary, for in some regions whole runs of salmon have been obliterated as a result of indiscriminate fishing. Nevertheless, it seems unfair that the coastal Indian, who has little or no opportunity of entry into other industries, and who still depends in large measure upon the salmon for his winter food supply should have to bear the privation which results from the white man's invasion of the coast.

What often happens is that the zeal of the local fishery officer inflicts great hardship on some illiterate Indian who does not understand the confusing regulations.

Maggie's man could not fish anymore, his arthritis confined him to the house. However, with the monthly pension cheque, the help of their grandchildren and the smoked, dried and bottled salmon which Maggie put up each year, they managed to live fairly comfortably. On a winter night when the Pentecostal service was held at their house and everyone was having a wonderful time "in the Lord," singing hymns and praying, Maggie could always afford to pull out a jar of rich, oily, sockeye to spread on hefty slices of homemade bread. She felt that it was the least she could do.

It was a good thing that she was still strong. Mind you, she puffed and wheezed quite a lot as she rowed the skiff down to the bay past the end of the village, and by the time she got the piece of net set and anchored with stones, she would have just enough energy to row back. Each day, once the net was set, she would row to the bay, work her way along the corkline watching for submerged floats, picking out the few fish. Some days there would be as many as a dozen.

It was a wonder Maggie's net caught any fish. The web was three seasons old and it was heavy number 53, not like the fine 43, 33, or even 28 gauge being used by the men of the fleet. Besides that, it was not the full twelve hundred feet in length. It was more like five hundred, not much of a net. But it was all that Maggie had, and after all she only wanted enough fish to put up for the winter.

One day Bertha came to the house. She was all excited and out of breath. Bertha was always out of breath, of course, because she was so heavy, but this time she really did seem to be upset.

"Maggie! Maggie! Maggie, don't go down to the wharf. That fishery man's down there with your net. Is he ever mad! He said you're not supposed to leave a net anchored like that. He tried to ask me who owned it, but honest-to-God, Maggie, I didn't say nothing. But he sure is mad. You should've seen him when. . . ."

Already Maggie was pulling on her wool sweater and heading for the door. When she got to the head of the wharf she saw the fishery officer. He was on the beach. A group of boys were standing about with their hands shoved into the pockets of tattered blue-jeans. Before him, piled in a heap, was Maggie's net. She watched him slosh the gasoline over it, saw him run a liquid trail away from the pile to act as a fuse. He chased the children further back, then he tossed the match.

Old Caleb was trudging up the ramp from the wharf. Behind him from the beach curled a genie of black smoke. He stopped in front of Maggie and their eyes met. They had been good friends for many years for Caleb and Maggie's man had fished together when they were young.

"I tried to tell him but he wouldn't listen," said Caleb. Then he went on along the boardwalk and turned into his house, and Maggie went to hers.

This story typifies the plight of many an up-coast Indian. One federal official burned an old woman's means of livelihood. During the winter another official would have to dole out relief money so that she could buy the less nourishing, highly expensive white man's canned meat.

None of the fish caught by an old Indian woman would be wasted. Yet during the heavy run of pink salmon in 1962, to take one example, thousands of whole fish were dumped back into the water by the fishermen because the canneries could not accommodate the catch. Is it any wonder that many elderly Indian people are bewildered, confused and resentful?

For the young men there are similar trials. Fishing is all that is known to the great majority of them. Their ancestors fished these waters. Their history is planted on the rugged shores as firmly as the mountains that look down upon the inlets. Their relationship to the salmon is historical, cultural and spiritual. It is intimate, far from the crass commercialism of the white man. Even if he did not have these strong ties to the fish and the sea, the paternalistic policies of a remote government have, until quite recently, had the effect of encouraging the Indian to remain on the reserve. The problem is that if he stays on the reserve the possibilities of earning an adequate living from fishing become more precarious with every passing season, and there are few if any other employment opportunities along the north coast.

Each year the number of people of other racial backgrounds joining the fishing fleet increases, while the Indian participation remains fairly constant at around two thousand to twenty-five hundred. The result is that an ever-diminishing percentage of the resource goes to the Indian, either as a direct supply of food or as a source of revenue.[2]

One of the most discussed problems related to the British Columbia salmon fishery today is this matter of overcrowding and the possibility of limiting licenses, though it is far from being a new problem. One fishery guardian wrote:

"Next season I think there will be a large increase in this number . . . but in my opinion, it is about time that some limit should be placed on the number of nets allowed on this river and I think the Fisheries Department cannot too soon take this matter into serious consideration."[3]

This was signed by John Buie and dated 1887. Over-participation seems to have been a problem from the inception of the industry. In fact, for a short period between 1889 and 1891 licenses were limited to five hundred on the Fraser River, a regulation which opened the way for all kinds of abuse and exploitation. Since that time, with the notable exception of Japanese Canadians, licenses have been available to any Canadian citizen who could afford the one dollar fee.[4] The Indian is the one who suffers most.

In 1883 there were three thousand and eighty-four fishermen in British Columbia, almost all of them Indians.[5] By 1962 the number had increased to over sixteen thousand with a little over twenty-three hundred being native.[6]

Although the increased number of licensed fishermen is a

hazard to the well-being of the Indian and to the existence of the salmon runs, the real threat comes from the increased effectiveness of the boats and gear being used.

Gone is the lonely hand-liner who stroked as much as forty miles a day in his open skiff. Around the kelp beds by Denman and Hornby Islands, up through Johnstone Strait or anywhere from Race Rocks to Prince Rupert the poor hand-liner pulled upon the oars and hoped for a box full of bluebacks, cohoes and springs. His equipment was simple. It consisted of four fathoms of cod-line, half a pound of lead, half a yard of piano-wire, a few fathoms of cutty-hunk, a number five brass "wonder" spoon and a free copy of the government tide tables. Under the bow in a box covered with a piece of oilskin was his double blanket, a frying pan and a battered coffee pot. If he snagged the rocks and lost his spoon he would have to row for miles to the nearest fish camp or harbour where he could borrow or procure a new one on credit and, if his credit was not good he might hack a piece out of the side of his coffee pot and shape it into a lure till he managed to get a few fish ahead. As night approached he climbed ashore, fried some bacon, ate a hunk of sodden bread and drank his black coffee. When it rained, as it nearly always did, the hand-liner crawled under his skiff for a few hours' sleep. At dawn he was off to the kelp-patches again, stroke, stroke, stroke through the morning fog, the noonday sun and the afternoon westerlies, with the line tied below his knee, hands curled into the shape of the oars, back bent, face scorched. It was a hard life, but a poor man could always scrounge enough pieces of equipment to go hand-lining, because the gear was simple.

Today, trolling is done from sophisticated vessels which can cost up to $45,000 to build and which come equipped with radio-direction-finder, echo-sounder, loran, automatic-pilot, radio-telephone and hydraulically operated "gurdies" which wind in the stainless-steel trolling lines, as many as eight of them, each with two or three sets of lures.

Similarly, gillnetting has advanced from the days when an Indian and his klootchman (wife) threw a rented linen net over the stern of a cannery owned skiff and waited till it was festooned with fish. Now nylon nets, owned by the fisherman himself and costing from $700 to $1,000 are run off the drums of high-powered boats that race from area to area hunting down the fish. If a fisherman wants to compete in the modern race for salmon he must have several nets varying in mesh size and colour depending on the species of salmon (Spring, Cohoe, Pink, Chum or Sockeye) and the water to be fished. The net that would be suitable for the Fitzhugh Sound area, for example, would not fish well in Rivers Inlet because the Inlet water is milky due to silt brought down by the river. A dark web would easily be seen by the fish during daylight, and they would simply dive beneath it or swim around. Furthermore, since the trend is towards a light gauge twine that will be less visible to the salmon, a web may not be used more than two seasons, three at the most. Many fishermen use a number 28 web valued at around $350 for only three weeks during the peak of the run, then they strip it off the cork and lead lines and throw it away.

In purse seining a similar situation pertains. Some of the more modern vessels ranging up to 90 feet in overall length cost as high as $350,000 though older seine boats would be valued at between $40,000 and $60,000. With a new seine-net costing up to $10,000 and shortened fishing seasons imposed as a result of the department's attempt to assure continued stocks, these larger vessels must find year-round fishing in herring, halibut and trawling for ground fish if they are to justify their existence economically.

What is happening, in fact, is that capital investment in Pacific Coast fishing has soared far past the point of diminishing returns. One dollar of invested capital in the prime industry which at the turn of the century brought a return of $5.37 in landed value in fish, based on the annual averages, in 1963 brought only 56c.[7] It has been said that 40% of the fleet could easily capture the full available amount of salmon.[8]

The ones who suffer most in this overcrowded situation are the Indians. They are being edged out of the only major industry open to them and robbed of their traditional source of food. No serious steps have been taken so far to insure that the shameful blunders which marked the advance of the white man across the rest of the continent will not be re-enacted on the west coast. Though competition has never been an integral part of the Indian's tradition, many have made the transition and are now numbered among the high-liners of the fleet. People around Alert Bay swear that the salmon follow Jimmy Sewid's seiner, that they fight to get into his net. Jimmy owns two seine boats, one of which he rents out, and the consistent high catches of this soft-spoken, discerning chief of the Nimpkish people is positively uncanny.

Up at Bella Bella for many years George Housty gillnetted sockeye in Spiller Channel so effectively that the fishery guardian was convinced he was robbing the creek under cover of darkness. George simply knew how to fish the area. He had learned from one of the old men of the village, and he was a worker. Numerous examples could be given to show that Indians are capable of competing in the harassing search for salmon that commences once the season opens.

But what happens to the average Native, the one who is *not* outstanding according to our standards — which ultimately may not be the best criterion but which, nevertheless, determine's one's relationship to the fishing industry as it is today?

The up-coast Indian is only three generations removed from the day when the whole coast was his to fish. In three generations the Indians have learned, with varying degrees of success, to accommodate themselves to the white man's world of money and machines, liquor and licensing, property and regulations. They have been subjected to the exploitation of the traders, the experiments of the government and the strictures of ultra-evangelistic Christianity. They fished for the canneries in the infancy of the industry before white men and Japanese came with their nets to share in the silvery wealth of the sea. Now their fishermen are outnumbered. Favourite drifts taught to them by their fathers are monopolized by the rapacious fleet from the big city and the jocund days when Louie Hall and his crew from the village of Klemtu could scoop up 47,000 humpbacks in one set are gone forever. Many inlets and channels that once teemed with fish, providing whole villages with food year after year, are closed indefinitely to fishing due to the near depletion of the stocks.

Once the Indian women worked in the draughty, shed-like canneries that cluttered the beaches and the bays. Now with centralization of the industry in a few major areas and perfected automation that can spit out 250 cans per minute from each of as many as five lines operating simultaneously, few Indian women are needed. Of course some of these changes had to come, but they leave the Indian bewildered, wondering where he can make a living if the trend continues.

Fishing is at best a precarious and seasonal source of income. Occidentals may join the fleet, end up as failures, and become easily absorbed again into logging, construction, industry or farming. But for the Indian of the coast there is no other industry. Consequently he may find himself an alien in his own land.

If he moves to the city where there is a variety of employment he suffers psychologically by being uprooted from the close-knit community of relatives and friends, and his natural surroundings as opposed to the ugly concrete desert of the city. He is adrift in a fast, frightening world for which he has not been equipped socially or academically. He must accept the burden of living in a society of money-grabbers and payment-pushers and he is inflicted with the anxieties of urban life, the threat of unemployment, eviction, hunger.

The Pacific Coast is perhaps the last area in Canada where the natural resource to which the Indian was originally attached is not completely obliterated or rendered useless. Throughout the rest of this continent the white man came with his guns and his greed. The forests were slashed, the stocks of fur-bearers were depleted, the herds of caribou and buffalo were slaughtered, and after the Indians were tutored to assist in the carnage till it was complete, they were pushed into little pockets of concentrated poverty.

Do not talk about the indolent Indian, his lack of initiative and lazy ways. If he is apathetic we have made him so by pillaging the only possibilities he ever had of being independent, the natural resources. If he is bogged down with ennui, we are to blame because we have pampered him with paltry hand-outs. The native North American was not lazy, indolent or irresponsible before the coming of the white man. He was a skilful hunter and fisherman. The lethargy with which he is so readily labelled by "civilized" society is the product of our half-hearted and indifferent tutelage. The wonder is that any natives have managed to emerge from the smothering avalanche of our insouciance.

On the West Coast the salmon runs are not yet annihilated and we have one last opportunity to show the Indian that we believe he is a person and that persons do matter more than money.

The question remains whether Canadians really believe this or not. If the present trend continues the Indian will be squeezed out of the fishing industry and little by little he will lose the right to find food from the sea. Then when we have taken away his natural food and his ancestral vocation, we will send in experts, white experts, who will teach him crafts. And then, having reduced him to a carver of curios which can be sold as authentic Indian handicrafts to tourists, we will demonstrate our charity and magnanimity by doling out relief. Only it will not relieve the misery of the salmon people.

CHAPTER 16

Thirteen Hundred Boats
for Sale - Cheap!

The injustice that was committed against more than twenty-two-thousand Japanese Canadians in 1942 was done under the Emergency Powers Act. In reality war with Japan was merely an excuse. It was the long-awaited opportunity for fear and ignorance to garb themselves in the uniform of feigned national interest, for the scalding hatred poured upon the Japanese people of the West Coast had been brewing in the pot of prejudice for fifty years. And the centre of this hatred was in the salmon industry.

"War would be a golden opportunity to buy up their property and ship them back to Japan,"[1] propounded one high official of the province prior to Pearl Harbour and when war came, sixteen-hundred Japanese-Canadian fishermen and their families, along with thousands in other occupations, were legally robbed of their boats and property, their homes and their hopes, and were shipped eastward to concentration camps or to work for token wages, denuded of rights and privileges. At the time, the manager of a northern cannery wrote to a friend in Vancouver, "Best thing ever happened the coast. They're crazy if they ever let the bastards back after the war."[2]

This was the prevailing attitude of Swedes, Norwegians, Finns, Czechs, Yugloslavs and Scots, Irishmen, Poles, Italians and Englishmen who had come to Canada, or whose forefathers had

THIRTEEN HUNDRED BOATS FOR SALE — CHEAP!

come from their respective homes looking for the good life in a land of freedom, natural wealth and opportunity, but who objected to people of Asian origin enjoying the same benefits.

Sixty-one percent of the Japanese-Canadians uprooted from their homes in 1942 were "Nisei", or Canadian born. Seventy-five percent were full citizens, and no cases of treason or disloyalty were ever found among them. However, since prejudice is incubated in ignorance no one seemed to consider these facts. The "Japs" as they were acrimoniously called, were hated because they held jobs and fishing licenses to which people of European stock, for some strange *un*-reason considered they had prior rights. The fact that many of the Japanese families had been in Canada for several generations longer than their accusers made no difference to the brittle-brained anti-Asiatic movement. It was hostility which had its origin almost as far back as the dawn of commercial fishing on the coast and which grew in tension as the intensity of fishing grew.

Manzo Nagano is reported to have been the first Japanese to reach Canada. He was a sailor, a restless adventurer who hopped ship when he landed in New Westminster in 1877, an offense which would have been punishable by death a few years earlier. For over two-hundred years Japan had been under the absolute authority of the Tokugawa Shogunate which carried out a programme of isolation so effectively that while explorations and discoveries were being made around the world, Japan lay locked in monastic-like seclusion. Only a few favoured Dutch and Chinese traders were permitted to enter her ports and no one was allowed to leave the country. The year of Canada's Confederation, Emperor Meiji came to power in Japan. Though Commodore Perry of the United States had negotiated a treaty providing for trade as early as 1854, it was not until the advent of the enlightened ruler Meiji that real fissures were opened in Japan's dyke against the world. Manzo Nagano's arrival in New Westminster was just nine years after Meiji's Charter Oath in which he proclaimed: "knowledge shall be sought throughout the world. . . ."

After Manzo Nagano hopped ship he managed to borrow a boat, and with an Italian as partner, fished the Fraser River out of Steveston. Soon he moved to Vancouver, then called Gastown, where he worked as a longshoreman. But the fever of adventure was in his veins and he could no more settle down than he could control the tides that lured him across the horizon. He sailed again for the Orient. When he returned to New Westminster in 1884 he discovered that seven or eight of his countrymen were fishing on the Fraser. Two years later he was fishing off the Washington coast when he was blown north by a violent gale. Once again he found himself at the mouth of the Fraser where he discovered that the handful of Japanese fishermen had grown to quite a sizable community.

Nagano did not settle in Canada till the year 1891 at which time he opened a small store in Victoria. Although he had been a wanderer, his first transient years around the Fraser marked the beginning of the Japanese Canadian community whose roots were to bleed from the biting axe of persecution as they fastened into Canadian soil.

Ironically, the year in which our friend Nagano settled in Victoria was the year in which the first attempt was made to restrict the number of Japanese immigrants through an amendment presented by a private member of the legislature. The Dominion Government disallowed the bill. But, the poison of prejudice was brewing and it was soon to spill over the rim of common decency.

On a Saturday evening early in June of 1893, Mayor Curtis presided at a public meeting held in New Westminster under the auspices of the Fishermen's Benevolent and Protective Association. The object of their diabolical benevolence was clearly indicated by the main speaker, D. F. Solmes, secretary of the Association, who pointed out the "injustices" suffered by the white fishermen because of the presence of Asiatics, and called for resolutions protesting the granting of fishing licenses to persons of Chinese or Japanese origin.[3]

It was a gathering which hewed the typical pattern for dozens

156

of others to follow, meetings at which articulate hate-mongers spewed incendiary words and ideas over a mob of like-minded listeners until resentment was stoked to the point of blazing anger. They wallowed in self pity. They worked themselves into a frenzy of fear and anxiety. With grotesque logic they talked themselves into irrational convictions about the future of the nation. They fed one another on fantastic tales of intrigue and insidious evil that supposedly festered within the Japanese community, and their discourses were lavishly punctuated with derogatory references to the breeding habits and ancestry of their Japanese Canadian neighbours.

It was inevitable after a few years of this sort of thing, goaded on as it was by the biased bleating of the Vancouver Daily World, that these Italians, Scandinavians, Poles, Yugoslavs, Czechs and Britons should carry their concern for a "pure" Canada out of the meeting hall into the streets, out of the realm of oratory into the sphere of club swinging for which they were admittedly better equipped by nature.

By 1899 the Japanese population at Steveston was around two thousand. Many of the men had sent for their wives and families. Others wrote home for "picture brides." In spite of the fact that initially some did return to Japan, it became obvious that the vast majority were settling down to make Canada home.

If the Japanese tended to remain separate from the rest of society it was not altogether due to language and cultural difficulties, for when people are spurned as a group they are forced to find solidarity among themselves. And so they settled in definite areas for the most part—Powell Street in Vancouver, Steveston at Fraser-mouth, Port Essington on the Skeena and eventually Ucluelet on Vancouver Island.[4]

Other racial and language groups followed a similar pattern. At Woodward's Slough and Sunbury the population was predominantly Finnish. Ladner was heavily settled by Yugoslavians. A strong community of Greeks was on Deas Island. Upcoast, Sointula on Malcolm Island was an abortive attempt on the part of some Finnish visionaries to form a communistic utopia, and Bella Coola valley was settled mainly by Norwegians looking for the good life. But in spite of this general pattern along the coast the presence of so many Japanese centred around Steveston and other localities was repugnant to the vast majority of Scandinavians, British and Europeans.

Still they settled. They came by the boat-load directly from Japan or via Hawaii. They came north from the United States where many had already tasted the bitter bread of hatred. They came and filled the demand for cheap labour on railroad gangs. They filtered into mining and lumber camps, and hundreds of them joined friends and relatives at Steveston, rented skiffs and nets and pushed out into the river to fish for the abundant sockeye. They did not have to learn English to fish and the life of a gillnetter, out on the waves alone or with his helper for the best part of a week, suited the stoical Japanese immigrant very well, for he would rather contend with the impartial fury of nature than submit to the humiliating abuse of brutish men whose qualifications for the superiority they claimed were based solely upon the colour of their skin.

Just as Yugoslavians tended to specialize in seining and Norwegians in halibut fishing, the Japanese gravitated towards gill-netting, probably on account of the independence it afforded. Because of their cohesiveness, their distinctive physical characteristics and perhaps most of all, because they were extremely hard workers, they were regarded as a hostile block of competition by practically everyone else. And the more their numbers grew the more they were resented.

In 1903 Victoria Trades and Labour Council memorialized Ottawa asking:

1. That no licenses for fish-traps, purse seines or gill nets be issued to Chinese or Japanese.
2. That no Chinese or Japanese be allowed to work on fish-traps, or with purse seines, or gill nets.
3. That Chinese and Japanese be excluded from working upon or taking part in the construction or maintenance of fish traps.

4. That no Chinese or Japanese be employed on any boat, scow or conveyance used in the transfer of fish from the traps to the place where the fish are canned or cured.
5. That persons securing fish trap licenses shall operate same within a reasonable time after said licenses have been granted.
6. And also that the Dominion Government should endeavour in some manner to encourage the employment of white labour more extensively in the canneries.[5]

This was the climate in which the Japanese immigrants found themselves once they were disgorged from the bellies of stinking ships onto the wharfs at Victoria and Vancouver. Still they came. They came seeking the right to work, to earn a living and to live in peace.

During the Russo-Japanese war (1904-05) the influx dropped sharply. Then, as the flow resumed, like pressure in some gigantic boiler the antagonism of the white population mounted until the inevitable happened. It was Saturday evening, September seventh, 1907 that Vancouver erupted into race riots.

Less than a month earlier the Anti-Asiatic league had been formed in the city. With an immediate membership of over five hundred they wasted no time initiating the pursuit of those aims and objectives inherent in their truculent title. A mass demonstration was organized, the highlight of which was to be the burning of an effigy of the Lieutenant Governor of British Columbia as a protest against employment of Oriental labourers at Nanaimo mines.

This lofty mission was preluded by a parade which would have been an ingenious masterpiece of ludicrousness, except that thousands of people took it seriously. Major Brown was marshal. He strutted through his brief, bright hour of glory revelling in the warm satisfaction of worthier causes subconsciously transferred to the present farce. When the convoy of carriages containing the officials of the league and their lady sympathizers finally moved off under his command, he swelled with misplaced patriotic pride as though he had just given orders to a battery of field artillery.

159

Behind the coaches in disordered waves that washed over the sidewalks came five thousand men on foot, bearing broad banners inscribed in garish colours with terse summations of the league's concern: 'WHAT SHALL WE DO TO BE SAVED? S.S. INDIANA WITH 1,000 JAPS DUE SEPT. 18TH, WE FOUGHT FOR THE EMPIRE AND ARE READY TO FIGHT AGAIN.'

Base causes have a habit of soliciting public sanction by enlisting the support of personages endowed with approved respectability and it is distressing with what ease this can be achieved. Thus, it is not surprising that among the speakers to address the crowd which milled about Vancouver's City Hall were certain members of the clergy.

The Reverend Dr. Fraser spoke impassionately, pointing out as he ascended to his rhetorical climax, that if something was not done, they would see even the pulpit in the hands of the Japanese and Chinese. The Reverend Charles H. Wilson made a somewhat quieter appeal. He called upon the mob to "solve the problem after the 'Christian' sense as would be commendable to the country," and hastened to explain that the best thing to do would be to "fill our country with our own kith and kin".

Meanwhile part of the mob decided to solve the problem in the only sense that could commend itself to their minds. Perhaps they took their inspiration from the affair two nights earlier across the border in Bellingham, where a mob had dragged numbers of Hindus from their beds, beaten and driven them from their homes. The speeches continued as from Dupont Street the crash and tinkle of broken glass could be heard. A rabble of hoodlums armed with bricks, stones and bottles rushed through the Chinese sector, smashing plate-glass windows, pelting doors with rocks and roughing up any of the inhabitants unfortunate enough to be caught out on the streets.

Like a great tidal wave the mob roared through the city, driven by hysteria. People who had come to watch the excitement found themselves caught up and swept along like drift. Soon they too were yelling obscenities, railing at the darkened

160

buildings or picking up rocks to hurl at windows. In front of the wave, like a destructive crest crashing upon some unprotected shore, a corps of wild young hooligans systematically smashed every plate-glass window of the establishments owned or operated by Orientals. On Columbia Street, apart from those of two white real-estate brokers, not a window escaped. Smithereens of glass spilled over the sidewalks and onto the streets where they were crunched under foot or kicked to and fro by the helter-skelter running of the mob which, having vandalized the Chinese quarter, swung into Powell Street ready to terrorize the Japanese. However, here the mob met with a surprise.

Word of the riot had raced through the Japanese community. Within minutes the men were armed with knives, ceremonial swords once deemed to be the soul of the samurai who bore them, bottles, clubs, stones, sticks, here and there a gun — whatever they could find. The surging rioters halted abruptly and fell back in fear as they encountered the silent wall of defense which seemed to be imbued with the ancient resolution of bushido.

For hours the noise and turmoil continued. There were a few skirmishes, some cracked skulls and some kicked ribs, but eventually Police Chief Chamberlin organized his men to throw a cordon across Carroll Street opposite the old "Woods" Hotel, and by 3 a.m. the city settled down to uneasy, watchful sleep.

Next day *Canton Alley* and *Shanghai Street* were packed with seething crowds of armed Chinese who, if it had not been for the persuasive words of Morikawa, their consul, would have spilled out into the city to seek revenge for the damage done the night before. By evening a mob began to form again. A few windows were broken and here and there scuffles occurred, but now the oriental communities were well armed and only the foolhardy would have ventured into range.

On Monday morning at nine-thirty, city solicitor Cowan headed out on a round of hardware stores imploring the proprietors not to sell fire-arms. Unfortunately the proprietors were human beings and therefore more easily persuaded by the pros-

161

pects of economic gain than by the will to maintain peace or to save life. It is one of those ironies of human nature that people who would gladly have seen the Asians run out of the country were ready to sell weapons to them simply because a profit was to be made. Within hours, in spite of atrocious prices, most of the stores from New Westminster to Vancouver were sold out of revolvers, rifles, axes, knives, pitch-forks, anything that would serve as a weapon. Private deals were made at black-market prices. One hotel-keeper sold a $10 rifle for $65. A revolver worth $6.50 went for $45. While opportunists made a few fast dollars, Powell Street, Columbia Street and vicinity became a virtual powder-keg with a short fuse of indignation that smouldered throughout the rest of the week. Very little provocation would have initiated bloody reprisals. A commission under the leadership of Mr. Mackenzie King was set up to investigate damages and make reparation. The political adroitness of this leader did much to asuage the anger of outraged Chinese and Japanese.

The demonstration and riot of that September accomplished nothing except the proliferation of hard feelings. One would think that with the boil broken the fever would have subsided. Such was not the case. Instead, white resentment continued to fester and to manifest itself in a wider set of symptoms.

Until the year of the riots Canada had been bound by the Anglo-Japanese treaty of 1894 which permitted any number of Japanese nationals to settle in Canada. In 1907 a gentleman's agreement was reached which provided that only four hundred Japanese should land in Canada annually. But Japan had no control over her subjects in Hawaii, so the number of immigrants continued to rise till by 1919 Japanese fishermen held some 3,267 licenses, nearly half the number issued in that year, and the peak of their participation in the industry.

Japan was an ally during the first world war. Indeed, quite a number of west-coast Japanese were in the Canadian Armed Forces for which they were rewarded in 1919 with federal enfranchisement. However, as service-men began to flow back into the fishing industry, and as the taste of victory and the hope for better times turned into the acid of disillusionment and discontent, it was the Japanese Canadians who once again became society's scapegoats.

Now the agitators worked mainly through politics. New anti-Asiatic organizations with absurd names such as, *The White Canadian Association,* brought pressure to bear on both the Provincial Legislature and the Dominion Government. In the decade following the first world war no less than five discriminatory resolutions aimed at restricting the freedom of Japanese were passed in Victoria. In salmon fishing there was a Japanese quota per district. Two hundred and fifty were allowed on the Skeena, fourteen on the Nass, seventy-two at Rivers Inlet and fourteen at Smith Inlet. Bella Coola had no quota and most of the remainder fished about the Fraser. They were not permitted to travel from one area to another in search of fish, as were other fishermen. Incredible as it seems, they were forbidden to have engines in their boats until 1930, an advantage enjoyed by whites and Indians since 1923.

The result of this ridiculous quota system was a form of corruption which made Japanese fishermen mere pawns in the hands of the unscrupulous. For example, on the Skeena the canneries divided the quota of two hundred and fifty so that each plant had a set number of Japanese delivering their fish exclusively to a particular company. When a new cannery came into operation the management naturally would want the services of some Japanese, for they were reliable and regarded as superior producers. Needless to say, the availability of Japanese fishermen under these circumstances became subject to the payment of certain unofficial fees which exchanged hands quietly and without signature behind drawn blinds.

Hiring of Japanese fishermen was done by the Jap Boss who received a rake-off, perhaps ½ c per fish, from each man for the privilege of fishing. When a Japanese fisherman drowned or died, his papers were placed in the cannery safe. The Jap Boss would receive as much as $75 for filling the vacancy and the new man would fish under the assumed name of the deceased.

In 1920 and 1921 the Dominion Department of Fisheries directed the Vancouver Fishery Commissioner to hold the number of licenses issued to Japanese at the 1919 figure. Then in 1922 the most cruel blow so far was struck. In that year a commission was appointed under the B.C. Fisheries Department to report on the problem of Japanese Canadians in the salmon fishing industry. Although no Japanese were invited to offer an opinion or to sit in on the hearings, the result was an immediate 33% reduction in the number of trolling licenses and a 10% reduction in gillnet licenses which was to recur annually until the Japanese were completely eliminated from the fishery.

This new hardship imposed upon the Japanese community can barely be imagined. From year to year they lived in anxiety, knowing that another 10% reduction in licenses would be made, each man wondering when his turn to be eliminated would come. Men who had worked hard, lived frugally over the years and saved strenuously until they eventually owned their own vessels, went to purchase the annual license only to be turned away, and the dejection carried back to the neat little houses at Steveston each season was not alleviated by the $300 granted from the local fund raised voluntarily to assist rejectees. White fishermen waited like vultures to buy their boats at rock-bottom prices and there was nothing to do but move out into new areas of industry, if they could find a job. Some twelve hundred persons were squeezed out of the industry this way even though the average Japanese had been in fishing for over twenty years.

Finally, by 1927 the Amalgamated Association of Japanese Fishermen sent representation to Ottawa to present the case of their people, and the reduction of licenses was arrested pending the outcome of the judicial battle that ensued. The Supreme Court rendered in favour of the Japanese and although the Dominion Government extended the battle, the decision was upheld by the Privy Council.

By 1929 the debris of discrimination seemed to be cleared. But the discretionary powers of the Minister of Fisheries was still used as a weapon to obstruct Japanese in the industry, so

164

that a year later a petition was sent to the Right Hon. W. L. Mackenzie King and to the Hon. J. P. A. Cordin, Minister of Marine and Fisheries, reading:

> "It is surely not British to accept a man as a subject, naturalize him, allow him to invest his capital in fishing gear, and after overcoming difficulties and learning to fish, push him out of it and practically confiscate his investment as a matter of political expediency. . . ."[6]

By the beginning of the second world war the struggle was still on. Premier Pattullo was baying at Ottawa to have restrictions imposed on Japanese fishermen again. Vancouver as late as 1941 passed a by-law requiring Orientals to live in their recognized communities, and most Occidental and Indian fishermen hated the "Japs". Consequently, the relocation during World War II was as much the culminating blow in a long history of hostility as it was the panicky response to Pearl Harbour.

Much has been written about the horrors of the relocation programme, the bewilderment and anxiety of the people, the discomforts and inconveniences, the emotional trauma suffered as a result of family dislocation, the pillaging and pilfering of goods, the vandalism, the carelessness of officials in disposing of property.

Over thirteen hundred boats, most of them gillnetters and trollers, were seized. Japanese of all fishermen took the most pride in their boats. Their vessels were symbols of their struggle to achieve economic independence and each spring as the Japanese fleet put to sea the sprightly waters put the spanking white and shining gum-wood hulls to dance. Now the owners saw their boats immobilized by removal of vital engine parts, saw them towed to assembly points along the coast where they were bashed together in rough weather and where thieves plundered them for instruments and parts. Many of the smaller craft sank with crushed hulls and owners who received payment of token values were fortunate, for in spite of the Japanese Fishing Vessel Disposal Committee, many received nothing at all.

It is not the purpose of this chapter to reiterate the economic atrocities nor to catalogue the indignities suffered by the Canadian Japanese during World War II, but to show that what happened in 1942 cannot be excused as the unfortunate result of war. That Canada's worst case of discrimination and racial persecution should have been born and bred in the fishing industry is a sad irony, for fishing has always been peopled by fierce lovers of freedom, men of keen competition and independent enterprise who share a healthy respect for the sea and an equally healthy contempt for many of society's superficial values. But in British Columbia commercial fishing was the breeding ground for prejudice, discrimination and persecution. It is a chapter most of us would rather forget, but without which the story would be inaccurate and incomplete, for Japanese Canadians were also a segment of The Salmon People, and now that over a thousand of them have filtered back into the fleet, they are still among the hardest workers and the top producers.

CHAPTER **17**

To Hell's Gate
and Back

It was a good year for fish in 1913, almost as good as the bonanza season of twelve years before. The fish which came up the Fraser that summer were third generation descendants of the 1901 run, since Fraser river sockeye usually live four years from egg to mature spawner. As the vigorous, healthy schools urgently entered the river en route to fulfill their destiny, no one suspected that tragedy lay in their path.

From early times it was an accepted fact that, for reasons unknown to man, the fish came in greater abundance every fourth year. Some fluke of nature had favoured the fish during one season, either providing a high level of ocean survival or advantageous conditions during the river migration. Perhaps in the obscure past some obstruction had blocked the progress of returning spawners for a few seasons, thus thinning the populations of those particular runs, but eventually clearing itself in the fourth year. Whatever the cause, the race of fish whose cycle years were 1897, 1901, 1905, 1909 and 1913 provided over sixty percent of the total catch in the twenty year period ending in 1916.

Fishermen and canners knew about this four year cycle so in the summer of 1913 every available craft was floated and a jocund spirit gripped the men whose boats plugged the mouth of the river and spilled out into Georgia Straits. Through July and into August the waters teemed with leaping, surging life and the morning mists that hung over the river were ripped with the sound of groaning oar-locks as heavy laden skiffs plied towards the cannery wharfs.

In from the mysterious paths of the ocean came the fish, wave upon wave, cutting the surface with their fins, flashing their white bellies at the sky as they drove inexorably on like a hoard of silent invaders. Into the river they headed. Individual fish now darted furtively, now glided with the tide, but always the whole body of salmon pressed onward, driven by an inexplicable determination to reach their spawning grounds, guided by mechanisms still a mystery to the human mind.

Thirty-seven million sockeye returned to the river that summer. Twenty-five million of them were strangled in the nets of the fishermen leaving what ought to have been ample numbers to spawn and thus insure a healthy harvest four years later when their progeny would return to the same gravel beds.

No wonder the Fraser was famous. With vast natural nurseries on eight major lake systems, not to mention numerous smaller streams where eggs were laid and hatched, Fraser was without dispute the greatest salmon producing river in the world, and the 1913 run seemed to be proving the point. However not many seasons later the assistant commissioner of Fisheries for B.C. was saying: "The Fraser is fished out. Its present condition is a monumental record of man's folly and greed."[1]

The runs never really recuperated from the crippling blow inflicted upon them that year and from the neglect which followed. At first it seemed like any other season except that there were more fish than usual. Those that were wary, or simply fortunate enough to elude the clutches of the fishermen's nets continued their tortuous upstream journey. There were fish headed for destinations seven hundred miles from the mouth, far up in the mountains on Francois, Fraser, Stuart and Takla Lakes. Others were headed for Quesnel and Horsefly lakes in the very heart of Cariboo country, or down the Chilcotin River into Chilko Lake under the frowning brow of Goodhope mountain. In normal years thousands would instinctively turn into the broad mouth of the Thompson, the Fraser's major tributary, and follow it to Kamloops Lake, Adams Lake and Shuswap Lake. But in 1913 few reached that far. Only those runs to Harrison, Birkenhead and Pitt lakes, which came later in the season and whose destinations were well below Hell's Gate where the tragedy occurred, went undamaged.

Hell's Gate! The place is well named. One hundred and twenty miles before it reaches the sea the Fraser gathers the water she has drawn from an area as large as the British Isles and pours it through a rocky funnel ninety feet wide. This is Hell's Gate, a savage cataract that grinds rocks beneath its surface and claws at the canyon wall with a roar that never ceases.

In 1913 the canyon resounded to other sounds; the clank and din of railway construction, the thud of dynamite, the crack of splitting rock, the shower of falling stones and the rumble of dumped debris. Millions of tons of rock blasted out of the mountain to make a bed for the rails had to be disposed of and in accordance with the methods of those whose primary aim is profit, it was dumped as close to the source as possible with little or no thought for the consequences. The result was that the gorge became narrower, the water swifter. Quiet pools where once the fish could rest in preparation for the supreme effort required to navigate the rapids were filled in, and as the 1913 runs entered the canyon, the waters plunged mercilessly down upon them.

Bravely the salmon pitted themselves against the torrent hugging tiny eddies, crowded out by other fish racing against the current only to become exhausted before another place of rest could be found, then swept downstream, often bashed to death upon the rocks by the ferocious river.

By the middle of August, immediately below Hell's Gate and for ten miles downstream, the river was choked with sockeye. But there was something strange about their behaviour. The usual dauntless determination of the fish gave away to pathetic lethargy. Frustrated, bewildered and fatigued, the ripening salmon milled about by the thousands in pools and eddies, their

169

backs now crimson, breaking the surface in a tired, pitiful rhythm of futility.

Even by the middle of September it was evident that their fate was sealed, for salmon embody nature's paradoxical balance of extravagance and strict economy. One female may lay as many as eight thousand eggs, but in order to do so successfully she must adhere to a strict time schedule. Her body is equipped with stored-up energy just sufficient to enable her to reach her home gravelbed at precisely the right time. Once there, travel-weary and bruised from the long journey upstream, she commences to excavate her redd. For several weeks with stubborn persistence she toils over the gravel until her tail is worn to a raw stump and death has etched its claim in figures of fungus about her head and back. Then she deposits her eggs in the eighteen inch deep nest, the male squirts his fertilizing milt over them and soon both male and female are swept away by the current to die. A delay of only a few days can upset the whole schedule. The fish may fail to reach the gravel before its allotment of energy is consumed and eight thousand units of potential life will be ruined. This is how it was with the major portion of the 1913 run.

As the days wore on the congestion below the rapids grew. Streams leading off the Fraser below Hell's Gate were plugged with spawning salmon, but their desperate depositing of eggs was futile. Often there was not enough gravel to cover the spawn and since the salmon egg is sensitive to temperature fluctuations their chances of survival in a foreign stream were negligible. Driven by confused instinct fish dug into what gravel could be found, only to disrupt the eggs of previous spawners. Thousands died without making any attempt to spawn at all.

From October to December the banks of the river were littered with the rotten carcases of several millions of fish that floundered without successfully laying their eggs, while upstream in areas where local settlers and Indians were in the habit of scooping out the passing fish, only a few were to be found. On the Anstey River an old settler and his two sons rowed a total of eighty six miles with their salt barrel, looking for fish. They saw only eight salmon where in previous years the river had been red with the driving hordes. On Skwa-am Bay at Adams Lake, where in previous big years the bar of spawned out, dead salmon could be gathered by the wagon load as fertilizer, only one male sockeye was found by the settler who came there annually.

But Hell's Gate was not the only cause of destruction to the Fraser River sockeye. The most famous salmon population of the Fraser system was the Adams River run. To get to the spawning grounds these fish unerringly turned from the torpid Fraser into the blue green water of the Thompson then on to the mouth of Adams River, three hundred miles from the sea. North through the Adams River they surged, into the long, high-cliffed lake and eventually into the upper Adams River with its thirty miles of gravel glistening under clear, cold water, perhaps the most valuable stretch of gravel in the world. In 1908 a logging company was permitted to build a splash dam across the upper Adams in order to flush their logs downstream several times a year. The result was devastating to the sockeye population. Even though a few fish managed to navigate the inadequate fishway that was eventually built past the dam, their eggs were gushed out by the destructive force of the water when the dam opened, or they were exposed to frost due to the disturbance of the water level.

This, combined with the Hell's Gate blockage, annihilated the Adams River run of sockeyes. The incredible stupidity of so-called civilized man, with his aptitude for destruction, had in a few years taken what nature and the Indians had maintained for centuries and rendered it almost useless. Nor was the Adams run the only one to be stricken.

On the Quesnel spawning system a similar fate befell the salmon. In 1898 a dam was constructed right across the path of the enormous schools of homing spawners and although it proved virtually useless for the mining operations for which it was originally intended, it was permitted to remain for twenty-three years. A diminishing number of fish managed to reach the spawning area each year until eventually the Quesnel run, which

171

used to be as high as fifteen million fish, dwindled to a mere fifteen hundred. The Quesnel dam in conjunction with the Hell's Gate obstruction, which by 1914 was made worse by a tremendous slide of rock and rubble loosened by blasting, practically obliterated this once magnificent annual run of wealth.

Another factor in the sad story of Fraser salmon was the rapacious trap and seine fishing of United States' concerns in Puget Sound which for years plundered the Canadian-bound fish as they swung south of Vancouver Island through U.S. waters. The trap was a deadly weapon against unsuspecting fish. A long fence-like obstruction called the *leader* extended from the beach perhaps half a mile, guiding the fish into a series of *hearts* and eventually to a *pot* from which there was no escape. From here, by means of the *spiller* the fish could be scooped onto a scow by the thousands to be delivered directly to the cannery. When Fraser River sockeye were plentiful it was not uncommon for a trap to capture as many as fifty thousand sockeye in a single day. Trap fishing was effective, but its indiscriminate use at strategic locations proved to be devastating to the runs.

As early as the turn of the century Canadian fishing authorities were concerned about the effects of U.S. traps in Puget Sound and Juan de Fuca. In the early part of the 1899 season for example, Puget Sound canneries were glutted with fish. Traps lured whole schools into their pots in such numbers that they suffocated and the weight of dead fish in many instances actually ripped the trap walls. Hundreds of thousands of whole sockeye were wasted. Dead and rotten fish were everywhere, while, on the Fraser only very modest catches were being made.

When Alexander Ewen and Daniel Munn heard about the catches in Puget Sound they decided to go and see for themselves. Sam Matthews, superintendent of Alaska Packers' Semiahmoo cannery received them hospitably, wined and dined them and escorted them on a tour of the cannery and the trap sites. What they saw made them tingle with excitement and expectation. The cannery wharf was filled to overflowing with bright, shining sockeye. Every scow they could find was crammed with

172

fish, and with extra help from the nearby town of Blaine the plant was operating an eighteen hour day. In fact the traps were so full that Matthews was going to have them opened to save them from destruction. To alleviate the glut he offered Ewen and Munn all the sockeye they wanted free of charge if they would provide their own scows and tugs. The Canadians declined. No sense transporting fish in scows, they figured, for within a couple of days the schools would be in the waters right off their canneries. They rushed home to prepare for the gigantic harvest. But the fish did not show up, and to this day that early run of sockeye has not been known on either side of the boundary. It was fished out.

Always the salmon's existence is under threat. Ling, suckers, squawfish and trout eat millions of eggs each fall. In spring when the inch-long alevins deplete their store of nourishment and their delicate egg sacs have disappeared they wiggle through the gravel and emerge as fry to be swept downstream into the icy water of the lake. Many of them are gobbled up by greedy trout. Even after a year of feeding on plankton in the lake, when they have developed into four-inch fingerlings headed for the ocean, they are vulnerable to predators, fluctuations in water levels, temperature changes and obstructions. But nature keeps her children in balance. Otter, mink, eagles, herons, loons, merganzers and grebes feed upon the ling, suckers, squawfish and trout. The original salmon people — the Indians — preyed upon them all, but never indiscriminately. They fished for food with respect, never destructively, never upsetting seriously the total balance of things.

Once the white man came with his guns and his greed, his whisky and his insatiable appetite for wealth the delicate harmony was broken and the valiant sockeye which had been returning to the rivers for thousands of years suddenly faced the gaping jaws of extinction. The white man is the salmon's greatest enemy.

Within fifty years from the time of James Syme's experiment on the kitchen stove back in 1867, as a result of the erection of

173

dams at crucial spawning locations, as a result of Hell's Gate and other obstructions, over-fishing on the Fraser itself and the deadly Puget Sound seines and traps, Fraser was reduced from the greatest salmon river in the world to an insignificant, average stream, no better in production than a number of smaller rivers along the coast. It appeared that what had happened on the Sacramento and the Columbia had finally caught up with the Canadian river.

It was in 1917 that the full impact of the Hell's Gate tragedy really became apparent. In that year the first generation descendants of the race that had been trapped below the rapids came back from their ocean travels, but their number was only one quarter that of the parent run. Efforts had been made to clear the Hell's Gate obstruction throughout 1914 and 1915 but the difficulties in accomplishing this task were gigantic and the impetus to do an adequate job was weak due to the opinion of some "experts" who were not convinced that serious damage was being done at that point. There was a myth prevalent in some circles that the salmon was invincible, that it could survive against almost any obstacle or hazard. Consequently, while the death toll rose year after year at the sinister narrows, rapacious fishing on the Fraser and especially on Puget Sound and Juan de Fuca Straits continued to plunder the weakening runs. By 1921 Fraser River sockeye had dwindled to sixteen percent of the 1913 run, and many canners and fishermen were already convinced the end of salmon fishing on that river was in view. Obviously the fish could not tolerate being assailed so mercilessly on so many fronts; at sea, in the river mouth and up the canyon.

Drastic steps would need to be taken if the sockeye were to survive. As early as 1908 Canada had been calling for an International treaty providing for the regulation of the fishery on either side of the border for the protection and nurturing of the salmon runs. But the bill failed to pass in the U.S. Congress due to influential commercial fishing interests in Washington State. For the next twenty years, in spite of repeated overtures on the part of Canada to enter into a treaty, the salmon lobby managed to keep the bill pigeonholed in the U.S. Senate. When the International Pacific Salmon Fisheries Commission was finally set up in New Westminster with three salaried officials from each nation, A. L. Hagar, first chairman of the commission who had worked so vigorously to bring it into being knew that the task before them was mammoth. The possibilities of reversing the trend and restoring the Fraser sockeye stocks were extremely meagre.

One of the first tasks undertaken by the commission was to determine the rate of mortality at Hell's Gate. Numbers of fish were captured and tagged. Later in the season it was discovered that the same fish, which normally might travel at the rate of from five to twenty miles a day, were still below the rapids. Apart from a few fortunate ones which somehow slipped through the torrent, the only fish that managed to negotiate the gorge in significant numbers were from a late fall run to the Shuswap area. They were able to pass upstream because the time of their migration coincided with a drop in the water level and a commensurate decrease in the velocity of the river. But some years, such as 1941, water levels remained difficult throughout the whole season. Then the fish died by the thousands.

By the time the sockeye commission had gathered sufficient data to proceed with remedial measures, it seemed to many of the fishery people it was too late. The wonderful days when "a fella could walk across the river on the backs of the sockeye" were gone forever and the industry was doomed. Indeed, if canners had not directed their attention to pink, cohoe, and chum salmon it would have collapsed completely. Today, even these species are showing the strain of heavy fishing. As for the Fraser sockeye, for over thirty years they had been subjected to slaughter by man and nature, and even though more stringent regulations had been imposed upon both Canadian and American fishermen since the formation of the international treaty, catches continued to be disheartening and the sustained low level of returning spawners indicated that there was little hope for the revival of Fraser sockeye, for everyone knew once the stocks reached a certain level natural enemies would complete the job of annihilation.

In 1944 work commenced on an imaginative fishway at Hell's Gate. For years studies had been made. Engineers designed an exact model of the canyon and the narrows, allowing water to flow through according to scale, studying the currents, the eddies and the velocity. Then they built a model of the projected fishway. It seemed good.

The actual project took two years and one million five hundred thousand dollars to complete. Finished in 1946, it consisted of two giant concrete flumes forty feet deep and one hundred and twenty feet long attached to the sides of the rocky gorge, and designed in such a way that a back eddying torrent would sweep the fish into the low velocity tunnel through which they could ascend in easy one foot leaps. The question was, would it work?

The 1947 runs were the first to use the new Hell's Gate fishway. That season yielded a meagre 450,000 catch. But now the Fraser was relatively free of blockages. The Quesnel dam had been removed in 1921 and the Adams River splash dam was demolished in 1945. Furthermore, when the main fishway was constructed at Hell's Gate three smaller ones were installed at up-stream rapids so that by 1947 once the fish entered the river, if they managed to elude the maze of nets about the mouth, they had only to contend with nature's normal culling process whereby she keeps the fittest of the species for reproduction.

When the progeny of 1947's spawners returned from the ocean in 1951 the catch jumped to two million, four hundred thousand fish, an increase of over five hundred percent. The hopes of the salmon people began to flicker once again. Three years later the catch, divided equally between United States and Canadian fishermen, ran up to ten million sockeye, the greatest run in more than forty years.

Then in 1958 fishermen and canners, government officials and members of the international commission were almost beside themselves with delight. For the sockeye returned to the river in numbers at least mildly reminiscent of the early days, though now on a different cycle. Eighteen million strong they came, the vast majority of them slipping down through Johnstone Straits, thus avoiding the U.S. fleet and giving Canadian fishermen the sort of bonanza that weds a man to fishing and gives him fortitude to face a dozen lean seasons. The miraculous had happened. The salmon had come back and the dollar value of one day's fishing in 1954 or 1958 would have paid for the construction of the fishways which had taken thirty-three years to become a reality.

The fish came back. But since 1958 there has not been another bonanza and what optimism there was a decade ago has been whittled down to a few slivers of hope, for the runs are still precarious, only remotely predictable, and the problems facing salmon and the salmon people are still multitudinous.

177

CHAPTER 18

Don't Go Near
the Water

They simply disappeared! Earlier vessels and aircraft had spotted the gigantic schools of fish off-shore. For miles the grey-blue surface of the sea had been flecked with twinkling specks of silver as the vigorous salmon sprang from the water to shake their magnificent bodies at the sun, and with the approach of the season's opening a fever of hope for another bonanza ran high among the men. On June twenty-seventh the *Vancouver Sun* reported that the fishing fleet was preparing for what was expected to be a mammoth harvest of sockeye. In False Creek, at Steveston, New Westminster and the dozens of little fish wharves and floats about the Fraser and on Vancouver Island, rigging was being repaired, nets were hung and last touches of paint were daubed upon hulls and cabins with the unique intimacy that exists between the fisherman and his boat. But the great run did not materialize. The season's catch turned out to be one of the most disappointing in the history of the industry and to this day the fate of the fish remains a mystery. The year was 1965.

It is like that with salmon. Although their normal life cycle is known and scientific studies continue to probe into the mysteries of their remarkable navigational powers, their breeding habits, ocean travels and general behaviour, every now and then, as though to arrest man's optimism, nature asserts her right to withhold her bounty for no apparent reason. And the salmon people are again reminded how precarious is the existence of the fish.

At the best of times nature is inexorably harsh. Land slides such as the one on the Babine River in 1951, when one hundred and fifty thousand cubic yards of shale, mud and boulders slid down the mountain side, can in one fell blow cause the death of hundreds of thousands of homing spawners.

Sudden changes in environment brought about by flood and drought are lethal to the tiny fry, the fingerlings in the lake, or the smolt on their seaward migration. In 1955, for example, floods deposited millions of fish eggs upon lawns and gardens by the banks of the Allouette River. Each time this sort of thing happens upon any of the thirteen hundred salmon spawning rivers and streams of British Columbia, countless numbers of fish lives are lost before they hatch.

Water temperatures are another crucial factor for the well-being of the spawning fish and for the orange-pink eggs once they are laid in the gravel. Horsefly River which rises in the heart of the Cariboo mountains and flows north-west into Quesnel Lake, has a normal temperature at spawning time of approximately 57 degrees. In 1963 three hundred thousand spawners which had escaped the talons and fangs of natural enemies, slipped through the labyrinthine jungle of nets and won the long, arduous battle against raging rapids and sharp rocks, finally reached their destination at the source of this river. But that fall there was an unusual warm spell. The water temperature at the gravel beds rose to 67 degrees and two out of every three fish perished.

The work of avaricious predators in lake and river and during the great migratory journeys extending thousands of miles into the North Pacific Ocean and the Bering Sea also imposes heavy mortalities. No one knows for sure how many fish are consumed by sharks, seals, sea-lions, killer whales and porpoises nor what other dangers lurk in the deep dark places of the immense salt-water world where the salmon spends more than half its life.

179

Sometimes a cloak of mystery conceals forever the cause of disaster. In 1956 there was a conspicuous failure of the cohoe runs to many Vancouver Island streams. Then, four months after the normal time of arrival local residents were surprised to discover the fish showing up in considerable numbers. They were battered and spongy, far from the firm, silvery specimens which usually arrived in late summer and fall amply fit to run the hazardous course up-stream. Yet with pitiful determination they were attempting to enter the rivers, even though frost and low water levels made the task impossible. Where had they been? What happened to them in the intervening four months? No one will ever know.

Even without unexpected catastrophies the future of the B.C. salmon population is dependent upon a slim margin. From three thousand incubated eggs possibly only one or two pairs of adult fish will return to spawn four years later.

Typical of the ways of white men with living resources, after plundering the salmon stocks greedily for half a century, authorities began to look about for the cause of the decline. Just as the wolf was blamed for the devastation of caribou herds, sea-lions and seals were singled out as culprits in the declining salmon stocks. In 1930 and 1931 the crew of the Fisheries vessel *"Givenchy"* gallantly massacred a total of 2,425 seal lions on summer cruises to the rookeries at Virgin and Pearl Rocks in Queen Charlotte Sound.[2] Indeed the foray was for a number of years an annual highlight of the crew's activities in the name of conservation.

In 1954 a gillnet fisherman in Rivers Inlet area was impressed with the number of fish he caught that bore marks of close shaves with hungry seals. He calculated that the number of fish escaping with mere marks of encounter must be considerably lower than those that would be actually eaten. His findings were reported to the fisheries officer and along with them he pressed the conclusion that the seals were threatening to deplete the salmon runs. He did not emphasize however, that he, as one of a fleet of several hundred gillnetters crammed into a relatively small area, had caught over one thousand Rivers Inlet sockeye in the space of three weeks.

But the real threat to the existence of the fish comes not from nature nor even from man's fishing activities, but from the careless by-products of civilization.

One of the most sinister and lethal dangers is that of pollution. Organic waste from sewage disposal systems, from meat, vegetable and fruit processing plants and from saw-mills overtaxes the capacity of the natural bacteria in the river or lake, the oxygen content of the water is disturbed in the process of decomposition, and the fish die. Inorganic waste from pulp-mills, mines and a variety of industries, not to mention insecticides and common household detergents are even worse. This kind of contamination could wipe out a whole population of fish within a few months. Methods are available for pre-treating waste so that purification is done before the effluent joins the river or stream. But the desire to minimize overhead costs in achieving profits often blinds industrialists to the harmful effects of pollution, making the work of the Provincial Pollution Control Board a matter of perpetual vigilance. The disturbing thing is that some authorities contend that pollution is inevitable, that it is the price we pay for civilization. If this is so, then perhaps the cost is too high.

From the beginning of settlement in British Columbia lumbering has been inimical to the fish. Much needless damage has been done by dragging logs through spawning beds, plugging narrow waterways with slash, building roads along the banks of streams or driving logs down shallow rivers. When the face of a hill is denuded of trees run-off may cause flash floods, temperature fluctuations in spawning areas, silting and erosion, all of which spell death to the salmon while in their delicate stages of development. Lumbering as the primary industry of the province must continue: no mistake about that. But whether it can be carried on with sufficient care to eliminate much of the senseless destruction to salmon stocks is still a crucial question.

One form of enterprise which certainly is incompatible with

181

sustaining salmon runs is the building of power dams. The eyes of those who are interested in hydro power have long looked upon the Fraser River covetously. A decade ago proposals were made for construction of a dam seven thousand feet high, and since that time a number of less spectacular proposals have been made. But if one of them comes into being it will be the end of Fraser River salmon, for to this day no feasible method of having power dams and preserving the fish in significant numbers has been found.

Suppose a major power dam were to be built on the Fraser. What would happen? Some mode of conveyance for transporting the fish to the higher level above the structure would have to be devised. This means that at the peak of a normal season it would need to effect the transfer at the rate of approximately thirty-thousand fish per hour, without delay and without damage, a problem for which there is no technical solution to date. In the spring hundreds of thousands of downstream migrants would have to be guided, collected and safely placed on the lower side of the dam. The possibility of thousands of young fish being chewed to pieces in the turbines or smothered against a screen, or destroyed by going over the spillway would be difficult to avoid.

If a dam were built the artificial lake thus created would pose perplexing problems for the salmon. Lack of current in this new environment, if they did manage to get into it, would bewilder the spawners, making navigation difficult or impossible. Some biologists believe that the salmon is guided by a very sensitive olfactory mechanism and that with the inundation of a vast area including the mouths of regular spawning streams the fish's ability to identify these streams would be impaired. Certainly many spawning areas would be completely flooded and rendered useless.

The problems are legion. With the creation of such a lake temperature barriers would be created and it is possible that many young salmon would not go to sea at all. They would remain in the reservoir. Normal food supplies would be disrupted, predation of coarse fish would be increased and oxygen disturbances due to decomposition of vegetation in the flooded area could bring stresses upon the stocks to which they could not adjust. The problems created by a major dam on the Fraser would be insuperable to the fish, even given the ingenuity of the salmon people to help them.

In the sporadic rounds of battle between vested interests of power production and those in the salmon industry a common weapon employed by the former is the contention that salmon fishing does not constitute a major economic factor in comparison with the value of power development; that sacrifices have to be made in order to pave the way of progress. Yet in a world where hunger and food production is a major problem, the possible destruction of an annual harvest of several millions of pounds of animal protein, a harvest that rivals and often surpasses the total annual beef cattle production of the Cariboo country, to endanger this resource for the sake of easy power would be an atrocity.

There are sources of hydro power on waterways other than the major salmon rearing systems. Let the power people exploit them. By the time they have been fully utilized atomic power plants will be at a point of perfection where they ought to commend themselves as an alternative to the ruin of an irreplaceable natural food resource.

United Nations, recognizing the critical state of expanding world population and food requirements, first sponsored a world conference on fisheries in 1955. Meeting in Rome, the purpose was to study ways and means of making the oceans and inland waters yield more fish for the world's food supply. Since that meeting studies have been conducted with growing urgency. With seventy-five percent of the globe's surface composed of water and only ten percent of the animal protein consumed by man now coming from the water, obviously man is going to have to look more and more to the seas for food. If this is so, then for Canada to allow her Pacific salmon to be wiped out by a few

183

kilowatt-hungry power pushers would be a crime against humanity.

There are problems related to the salmon's life in fresh water, to be sure, but at least this is Canadian water and Canada can, if it will, determine what steps are necessary to insure the continuation of the runs. However, once the fish are in the Pacific and beyond the 12 mile fisheries zone, they are fair game for the fleets of the world. Herein lies one of the most perplexing problems facing the salmon and the salmon people today.

Canadians eat approximately fourteen pounds of fish per person per year. In United Kingdom the figure is between forty-five and fifty-five pounds. In Japan, however, annual fish consumption averages around ninety pounds per person. Japan, with its ninety millions of people crammed onto four small islands, must look to the seas for food.

Until June 1964, the North Pacific Fisheries Convention, signed ten years previously by United States, Japan and Canada, restricted Japanese fishing fleets to the waters west of the 175th meridian. The result was they fished vigorously in those areas left open to them. In the early fifties the Japanese commenced a programme of high seas fishing which jumped from two million fish in 1952 to fifty-eight million in 1955.

Russia was outraged. Their Siberian salmon fishery conservation schemes were being shattered. In February 1956 they barred the Japanese from fishing in the Sea of Okhatsk, the western Bering Sea and the north-west Pacific, claiming that salmon in these waters were reared in Russian territory and that they had a right to protect their interests. Whether or not they had a right it soon became apparent that they meant business, for when some Japanese vessels ventured into the region of Kuril Islands they were promptly fired upon by Russian patrol boats. Meanwhile, west and south of Japan, Korea was building a magnificent fleet of her own by confiscating Japanese boats that strayed across an imaginary line in the ocean. Peru and Ecuador have claimed exclusive fishing rights one hundred and fifty miles off shore, and they back their claim with gun boats, while Australia has warned the wandering Japanese fleets to stay clear.

Once the North Pacific Fisheries Treaty expired in 1964 Japan, quite naturally, refused to renew it. She needs fish desperately and since Canada seems to be, of all nations, the least concerned about the resource reared in her rivers, there is little wonder that huge mother ships with their fleets of trawlers, tankers and freighters of both Japanese and Russian origin, are being sighted with increased frequency just off the British Columbia shores.

Neither Japan nor Russia hesitate to act when what they consider to be their own fisheries resources are threatened by foreign interests. Recently sixteen Japanese trawlers fishing eighteen miles offshore from Primorskii Kraii (the Soviet Maritime Region of Siberia) in the Japan Sea were ordered out of the sea by a Soviet patrol boat. Japan has closed her ports to foreign fishing vessels and established a twelve mile limit off the five prefectures bordering the Japan Sea. Since 1964 Canada too has claimed three miles territorial limit and an additional nine mile exclusive fishing zone, but the problem has been in establishing a realistic base-line from which to measure the total twelve mile limit. As it stands now, twelve miles from the base line allows foreign vessels to scrape the ocean floor just off the shores of Vancouver and Queen Charlotte Islands.

Not only is the proximity of foreign fleets a threat to the stocks of salmon, many of which are immature when captured, but the resultant competition in the world market plays havoc with Canadian customers. Russian and Japanese fishing operations tend to be more economical than Canadian. They are not harassed by escalating wage demands to the same degree, and the practice of fishing, canning and shipping right from a factory ship on the grounds eliminates much overhead. The result is that traditional markets such as South Africa, Australia and Great Britain are being forced to take a hard look at the value of continuing to purchase from Canada.

And so salmon fishing in British Columbia is a problem-infested industry in which conflicting interests upon the inland waterways threaten to spoil the source of wealth forever, an industry in which tender international relations plague the possibility of adequate protective policies, in which bitterness between the United Fishermen and Allied Workers' Union, the Pacific Trollers' Association, the Fishery Vessel Owners' Association, the Prince Rupert Co-operative Association and the B.C. Fisheries Association has blemished season after season with senseless and expensive strikes. It is an industry in which the unpredictable whims of nature continue to wreck fortunes, ships and lives and where a massive fleet of trollers, seiners and gillnetters with highly effective gear vie with one another and with nature in furious competition for the fish.

The future is uncertain. It is true that an imaginative campaign has been launched by the Federal Department of Fisheries, the International Pacific Salmon Fisheries Commission and smaller committees such as the Skeena Salmon Management Committee and the Johnstone Strait Management Committee, all devoted to the maintenance of favourable conditions for the maximum annual return of the various species of salmon. Since the first one at Hell's Gate, fishways have been constructed at difficult navigational points. Artificial spawning channels and rearing stations are adding a new dimension of hope for the restoration and maintenance of some runs, while watchful conservation affords the fish protection from outright depletion from fishing or stream spoilage. Yet the overall picture leaves little room for rejoicing. The annual runs in recent years have fluctuated from a high of $37 million landed value in 1958 to a low of $18 million just two years later. The future of the salmon remains unpredictable.

It is a problem-plagued industry and the best advice to anyone thinking of entering it would be, "Don't go near the water!" Yet those who have seen the thrashing silver in a gillnet or caught the bubbles in the circle of a seine or hauled the metallic bright cohoe and spring salmon into the stern of a troller know the rhythm of the sea's roll, the whip-sting of salt spray from a crashing bow, the great solitude of being wrapped in morning mist, the fearsome scowl of a stormy sky. They know the exhilaration of a fatigued body and jubilant spirit as they pitch the last of a bonanza catch to the deck of the collector. They know the smell of coffee and steak that lies in layers about the weekend fish camp, and they would not exchange these things for the time clock and the late afternoon traffic jams. They are the salmon people. And so are the men and women who work amid the din and clank of the cannery and those who fuss over the daily pack or worry through the winter bartering half way around the world to sell the bright pink flesh. So are the men in green uniforms who patrol the waters and guard the creeks to see that next year there will be salmon again. They are all salmon people, all watching and waiting and hoping for the wary fish in their own way.

The coast has changed since the days of the stoical native quietly storing up his winter food, or since the rough-hewn pioneer canner who pulled fast fortunes from the inlets and the bays. The lonely hand-liner dragging crude lures beside the kelp patches is gone now and so are most of the grey, weather-worn canneries. The old community spirit of up-coast when cluttered steamers groaned against the cannery wharves unloading paraphernalia and picking up gossip, seems to have disappeared. Today a sophisticated harshness holds the salmon industry in its grip and uncertainty strums upon the nerve chords of the canners, the shoreworkers and the fishermen alike.

But so long as there are fish surging in from the sea there will be salmon people willing to brave the torments of nature to catch them, and the salmon will probably come forever . . . if man does not destroy them.

Chapter Notes

Chapter 1
1. This is a synthetic story based on the first salmon ceremony as described by Erna Gunther in *"Analysis of the First Salmon Ceremony"*; American Anthropologist, New Series, Vol. 28, No. 4, Wis., U.S.A., 1926.

Chapter 2
1. BOAS, Franz: *"Ethnology of the Kwakiutl"*, 35th Report of Bureau of American Ethnology, 1921, p. 1318-1319.
2. BORDEN, Charles E.: *"Fraser River Archaeological Project"*, National Museum of Canada, No. 1, Dec. 29, 1961.
3. HARMON, Daniel W.: *"Journals of Travel"*, A. S. Barnes and Co. Ltd., N.Y., 1903, entry for Aug. 2.
4. Ibid. Entry for Thursday, August 22.
5. Ibid. Entry for Saturday, August 15.

Chapter 3
1. WILSON, Jack: *"The Sockeye in History"*, Chase Centennial Committee, 1958.

Chapter 4
1. This book first published by Appert in 1910 became a popular kitchen handbook for many years. See HEDGES, E. S. *"Tin in Social and Economic History"*, Arnold, London, 1964.

Chapter 5
1. Oolichans, sometimes called "Candle Fish" because of their extremely high oil content, are small, smelt-like fish which annually migrate by the millions to spawn in certain rivers of the coast. They are rendered into oil by the Natives. The oil is highly valued as an article of barter and lamp fuel (in earlier times), a cooking ingredient, medicine, or simply as a dressing.
2. British Columbian, May 9, 1862, p. 2.
3. Colonist, January 15, 1869.
4. Ibid, April 20, 1881, p. 3.
5. There were by this time about three-hundred farms of 1,200 or more cultivated acres in the Fraser Valley.
6. Colonist, June 28, 1864.

Chapter 7
1. Report of the Commissioner of Fisheries, 1877, Victoria, B.C.
2. British Columbian, May 31, 1882.
3. Canada Sessional Papers, 1893, No: 10c p. 229.
4. Ibid, p. 170.

Chapter 10
  1. Doyle Papers, U.B.C. Special Collections, Vancouver, B.C.

Chapter 12
  1. LARGE, R. W.: *Missionary Bulletin*, Volume 2, #1, 1904, U.C. Archives, Victoria University, Toronto, Ontario.

Chapter 13
  1. For the full story of this man's career see McKervill, Hugh W. *"Darby of Bella Bella"*, Ryerson Press, Toronto, 1964.

Chapter 15
  1. This is a true story though for obvious reasons the names are fictitious.
  2. Federal-Provincial Committee on Wage and Price Disputes in B.C. Fishing Industry: *"A Summary Review etc."* Nov. 1964, p. 64, Tab. 28.
  3. CAMPBELL, BLAKE A., *"The Role of the Fisherman in the Economy of British Columbia"*. Address presented at B.C. Natural Resources Conference on March 3, 1961, Vancouver, B.C., p. 3.
  4. In 1966 this was raised to $5 with an additional $10 boat registration fee, plus a $5 salmon fishing boat license fee, $20. The increase was designed to discourage casual fishing.
  5. CAMPBELL, BLAKE A. Ibid, p. 4.
  6. Federal-Provincial Committee, *"Summary Review"* p. 64, tab. 28. It must be borne in mind that a considerable number of licenses are held by "moonlighters", or part-time fishermen.
  7. Ibid, p. 57, tab. 25.
  8. Correspondence with Provincial Department of Fisheries, Victoria, B.C., 1966.

Chapter 16
  1. Toronto Star Weekly: September 20, 1941.
  2. Inverness Papers, U.B.C., Special Collections, Vancouver, B.C.
  3. Vancouver Daily World. June 7, 1893, p. 8.
  4. In 1917 six Japanese fishermen moved to Ucluelet. This marked their entry into trolling. By 1926 their numbers had increased to the point where they were successful in organizing the West Coast Trolling Fishermen's Association.
  5. Letter and memorial by Victoria Trades and Labour Council, Victoria, B.C., 16th of March, 1903, Public Archives, Ottawa.

6. Petition to Rt. Hon. W. L. Mackenzie King and Hon. J. P. A. Cordin, Minister of Marine and Fisheries, Ottawa, February 1930, by Citizens of Canada of Japanese Origin, in Provincial Archives, Victoria, B.C.

Chapter 17

1. Canadian Fisherman, Vol. 10, p. 101, June 1920.

Chapter 18

1. See appendix on Life Cycle of Salmon.
2. Fisheries News Bulletin, Department of Fisheries, Volume 11, #22, August 1931, p. 3.

Selected Bibliography

General

Beard, Harry R., *The Story of Canfisco,* Canadian Fishing Co. Ltd., Vancouver, B.C., 1937.

Blake, W. H., *A Fisherman's Creed,* Toronto, MacMillan Co., 1923.

Borden, Charles E., *Fraser River Archeological Project,* National Museum of Canada Series, No. 1, December 29, 1961.

Burdis, W. D., *Treatise on British Columbia Salmon,* Vancouver, B.C., Salmon Canners Association, 1922.

Carrothers, W. A., *The British Columbia Fisheries,* Toronto, U. of T. Press, 1941.

Davis, Horace, *Record of Japanese Vessels Driven Upon the N.W. Coast of America,* Worchester, Mass., Chas. Hamilton, 1872.

De Voto, Bernard, ed. *Lewis & Clarke, Journals* of, Boston, Houghton, Mifflin Co., 1953.

Drucker, Philip, *Cultures of the North Pacific Coast,* San Francisco, Chandler Publishing, 1965.

Duff, Wilson, *The Indian History of British Columbia,* Anthropology in British Columbia, Memoir No. 5, Volume 1, "The Impact of the White Man", Provincial Museum of B.C., Victoria, 1964.

Fisheries Association of B.C., *Salmon, the Living Resource,* Vancouver, 1966.

Gunther, Erna, *Analysis of the First Salmon Ceremony,* American Anthropologist, New Series, Wisconsin, 1926, Vol. 28, No. 4.
A Further Analysis of the First Salmon Ceremony, Publications in Anthropology, University of Washington Press, 1928, Vol. 2.

Haig-Brown, Roderick L., *Return to the River,* Vancouver, 1946.

Harmon, Daniel W., *Journals of Travel,* New York, Barnes and Co., 1903.

Hawthorn, Belshaw and Jamieson, *The Indians of B.C.,* Toronto, U. of T. Press, 1958.

Hedges, E. W., *Tin in Social and Economic History*, London, Arnold, 1964.

Hutchison, Bruce, *The Fraser*, Toronto, Clarke Irwin Co. Ltd., 1950.

Jewett, John R., *The Adventures and Sufferings of*, Edinburgh, 1924.

Kerr, J. B., *Biographical Dictionary of Well-Known British Columbians*, Vancouver, Kerr and Begg, 1890, p. 163-64f.

Larkin, Peter, *Fish Power Problems*, H. R. MacMillan Lectures, U.B.C., 1957 (published 1958).

Mackintosh, C. H., *Potential Riches of B.C.*, British American Trust Co.

MacMillan, H. R., *Printed Historical Sketches of Plants in B.C. Packers*, Provincial Archives, Victoria, B.C.

May, Earl Chapin., *The Canning Clan*, N.Y., MacMillan Co., 1937.

Morice, Rev. A. G., *Fifty Years in Western Canada*, Toronto, Ryerson Press, 1930.

Morley, Alan, The Lonely Hand Liner, in Water's R. E. *B.C. Centennial Anthology*, 1958, p. 139.

Netboy, Anthony, *Salmon of the Pacific Northwest*, Portland, Oregon, Binfords and Mort, 1958.

Newcombie, M. C. F., *Menzies Journal of Vancouver's Voyage April to October 1792*, Victoria, 1923.

Nicholson, George, *Vancouver Island's West Coast, 1762-1962*, Victoria, B.C., 1962.

Ormsby, Margaret, *British Columbia, A History*, MacMillans of Canada, 1958.

Ramsey, Bruce, *Ghost Towns of British Columbia*, Vancouver, Mitchell Press, 1963.

Reid, Robbie L., "Economic Beginnings in B.C.", *Royal Society of Canada Record of Proceedings*, 1936, Third Series, Vol. XXX.

Taylor, Gordon, *"Delta's Century of Progress"*, Delta Centennial Committee, 1958.

Wallace, F. W., *"Prince Rupert and its Future"*, Pacific Coast Fisheries, Toronto, MacMillan & Co., 1916, p. 303-308.

Young, H. and Reid, H. R. Y., *The Japanese Canadian*, Toronto University Press, 1938.

Government Publications

Alexander, G. J., *Commercial Salmon Fisheries of B.C.*, Provincial Department of Fisheries, Victoria, 1947.

Biological Board of Canada, *Artificial Spawning Methods for Sockeye Salmon*, Bulletin #50, 1936.
Biological Board of Canada, *Tagging of Sockeye Salmon*, Bulletin #2, 1929.

Campbell, Blake A. and Young, S. L., *Fishing Returns in British Columbia*, Department of Fisheries, Vancouver, March 1966.
Campbell, Blake A., *The Role of the Fisherman in the Economy of British Columbia*, Department of Fisheries, Vancouver, B.C., 1960.
Canadian Parliament, House of Commons, *The Washington Treaty Debate*, Reprint from "Daily Mail" (supplement), Toronto, June 1872.
Clemens, W. A., *Some Historical Aspects of the Fisheries Resources of British Columbia*, reprint from 9th Natural Resources Conference Transactions, February 1956.
Cooper, A. C. and others, *History of Early Stuart Sockeye Run*, International Pacific Salmon Fisheries Commission, Report #10, New Westminster, 1962.

Department of Fisheries, *News Bulletin*, August 1931, Volume 11, #22.
Dyson, J. B., *The Babine Rock and Earth Slide*, Federal Department of Fisheries, Ottawa, 1947.

Foerster, R. E., *The Effect of Power Dams on Pacific Salmon*, Fisheries Research Board of Canada, September 24, 1952.
Federal-Provincial Committee on Wage and Price Disputes in the British Columbia Fishing Industry, A Summary Review, November, 1964.

Godfrey, H., *Babine River Salmon After Removal of Rock Slide*, Fisheries Research Board of Canada, Ottawa, 1956.

Haig-Brown, Roderick L., *Canada's Pacific Salmon*, Department of Fisheries, Ottawa, 1956.

International Pacific Salmon Fisheries Commission, *Salute to the Sockeye*, New Westminster, 1958.

Japanese Fishing Vessel Disposal Report, Provincial Archives, Victoria, B.C., 1942.

Killick, S. R., *Chronological Order of Fraser River Sockeye Salmon During Migration, Spawning and Death,* International Pacific Salmon Fisheries Commission, Bulletin VII, New Westminster, 1955.

Peterson, Alvin E., *Selective Action of Gillnets on Fraser Sockeye,* International Pacific Salmon Fisheries Commission, Bulletin V, New Westminster, 1954.

Pritchard, A. L., *Findings of the British Columbia Pink Salmon Investigation,* Fisheries Research Board, Part III, 1938.

Report of Special Fishery Commission 1917, Ottawa, King's Printer, 1918.

Thompson, W. F., *Effect of the Obstruction at Hell's Gate on the Sockeye Salmon of the Fraser River,* International Pacific Salmon Fisheries Commission, New Westminster, 1945.

Thompson, W. F. and Talbot, G. B., *Biological Report on Hell's Gate Obstruction,* International Pacific Salmon Fisheries Commission, New Westminster, 1943.

Walbran, John T., *Place Names of the B.C. Coast, 1592-1906,* Government Printing Bureau, Ottawa, 1909.

Manuscript Sources

Bancroft Papers, C. Series, Numbers 2, 6, 9, 11, 12, 13, 15, 16, 17, 20, 21, 23, 24, 26, 29, 32. Public Archives, Ottawa.

Brewster, H. C., *Correspondence With Clayoquet Sound Cannery Co. Ltd., 1870-1918,* M.S. in Provincial Archives, Victoria, B.C.

Charmichael, Alfred, *An Account of a Season's Work at a Salmon Cannery,* M.S. in Provincial Archives, 1891.

Compton, P. N., *Account of Early Trip to Fort Victoria and of Life in the Colony,* Provincial Archives, Victoria, B.C.

Doyle, Henry, Uncatalogued Papers, Special Collections, U.B.C.

Fort Langley Journal, 1827-1831, Victoria Archives.

Gibbard, J. E., *Early History of the Fraser Valley, 1818-1888,* Thesis, U.B.C., 1937.

Gladstone, Percy H., *Industrial Disputes in Commercial Fisheries of B.C.,* Thesis, U.B.C., 1959.

Hacking, N., *Early Marine History of British Columbia,* Thesis, U.B.C., Vancouver, 1934.

Hewes, Bordon, *Aboriginal Uses of Fisheries Resources in N.W. North America,* University of California, Barclay, 1947.

Inverness Papers, Uncatalogued papers, Special Collections, U.B.C.

Laurier Papers, Public Archives, Ottawa, Numbers 126246, 59569-70, 70711-12, 72661, 86022.

Lawrence, Joseph C., *An Historical Account of the Early Salmon Canning Industry in British Columbia 1870-1900.* Thesis, U.B.C., 1951.

Loder, Austin, *Correspondence Out,* August 1893, two letters in Provincial Archives, Victoria, B.C.

MacKenzie, Alex., *Memorandum—Varieties of Fish in Skeena River and Queen Charlotte Sound,* M.S. Provincial Archives, Victoria, B.C., 1879.

McDonald, Archibald to Ermatinger, *P.A.B.C. McDonald Papers, Correspondence Out,* February 20, 1831.

McDonald, Archibald and Others, *Fort Langley Correspondence,* from the Archives of the Hudson's Bay Company, 1830-1859, Provincial Archives, Victoria, B.C.

McTavish, George S. M., *Fifty Years Ago in the Canning Industry,* M.S. in Provincial Archives, Victoria, B.C., 1941.

Mitchell, Davis S., *The Story of the Fraser River's Great Sockeye Runs and Their Loss,* M.S. Provincial Archives, Victoria, B.C., 1925.

Ralston, Harry Keith, *The 1900 Strike of Fraser River Sockeye Salmon Fishermen,* Thesis, U.B.C., Vancouver, 1965.

Stevens Papers, Public Archives, Ottawa, Volume 58, 97.

Strong, Gordon, *The Salmon Canning Industry in B.C.,* Thesis, U.B.C., 1934.

Sumida, Reginald, *The Japanese in British Columbia,* Thesis, U.B.C., Vancouver, 1934.

Swan, J. G., *Correspondence Out 1818-1900,* Provincial Archives, Victoria, B.C.

Periodicals

British Columbia Digest, December 1945, Volume 1, #1, p. 7.

Canada Sessional Papers, 1893, No. 10c p. 229, and p. 170.

Campbell, S. K., "The Fisheries of British Columbia", *The Caduceus,* October 1925, Volume VI, #3, p. 18f.

Gladstone, Percy and Jamieson, "Unionism in the Fishery Industry of B.C., *Canadian Journal of Economics and Political Science*, May 1950, Volume 16, #2, p. 156.
Green, Ashdon Henry, *Natural History Society of B.C.*, 1891, Volume 1, No. 1, p. 20-33.

Kalehmainen, John J., "Harmony Island, a Finnish Utopian Venture in B.C., 1901-1905", *British Columbia Historical Quarterly*, Victoria, 1941, Volume V, #2, p. 111.
Kraft, R. W., "Investigations of the Effect of the Power Development On Fisheries", *Engineering Journal*, November 1954, Volume 37, p. 1446.

Luce, P. W., "Fishy Business", *Maclean's Magazine, March 1, 1937*, 50: 19.
Lyndell, Honorie B., "Salmon Trollers of the Pacific", *Maclean's Magazine*, July 15, 1932, Volume 45, p. 15.

Mahaffy, R. V., "Pacific Salmon Commission Lodges Case Against Dams", *Canadian Fisherman*, July 1955, Volume 42, p. 23.
Marine Life, Vancouver, B.C., 1909, Volume 1, No. 1.
McDonald, Archibald, "Letter to Friend", *Washington Historical Quarterly*, Volume 1, p. 258-260, 1906-07.

Olsen, W. H., "Marked for Life," *B.C. Digest Magazine*, January 1946, Volume 1, #2.

Pioneer Salmon Cannery Labour Contractors, Western Fisheries Magazine, June 1936, p. 9.
Pritchard, A. L., *Skeena River Salmon Investigation*, Reprint from Canadian Geographical Journal, August 1949.

Swan, L. G., *A Century of B.C. Fishing*, reprinted from "Trade News", Department of Fisheries of Canada, Ottawa, April 1958.

Weston, G., "Steveston By the Fraser", *British Columbia Magazine*, 1911, p. 776 f.

Yonemura, Hozumi, *Japanese Fishermen in B.C.*, Canadian Forum, July 1930.

Newspapers

Daily Colonist, Copies from 1859—at Provincial Archives, Victoria, B.C.

Northern Star, Prince Rupert, B.C., August 29, 1947.

Prince Rupert Daily News, Special Fishing Edition, Prince Rupert, August 30, 1963.

The Fisherman, Copies from 1937—at United Fishermen and Allied Workers Union Office, Vancouver, B.C.

Vancouver Province, copies from 1898, U.B.C., Special Collections, Vancouver, B.C.

Vancouver Sun, copies from 1886 in Provincial Archives, Victoria, B.C.

Vancouver World, copies from 1893-1908, U.B.C., Special Collections, Vancouver, B.C.

Western Fisheries, Bound copies from 1929, Vancouver, B.C.